MUSLIM EDUCATION IN MEDIEVAL TIMES

BAYARD DODGE

Qadeem Press

Qadeem Press

Qadeem Press Edition
Breathing Life into Forgotten Pages
www.qadeempress.com

Find our titles on your favourite online bookstore using the keyword 'Qadeem Press'

Contents

PART I

PART II

DEVELOPMENT OF THE SUBJECTS OF THE CURRICULUM

Foreword

While students are studying medieval education, they too often forget that side by side with Latin learning there existed a flowering of Arabic culture, which held sway from Spain to Afghanistān, making important contributions to the European Renaissance. It is hoped that the brief account given in the following pages will help a student, who is unable to read Arabic, to appreciate what the schools and studies of the Muslim lands were like.

I am exceedingly grateful to Professors Ishak Husaini of the American University at Cairo, Farhat Ziadeh of Princeton University and Habib Amin Kurani* of the American University of Beirut, as well as to Edwin E. Calverley and Elmer H. Douglas of the Hartford Seminary Foundation, for reading my manuscript and giving me generous help.

BAYARD DODGE

* These names are spelled as they are written by the professors themselves, rather than according to the transliteration system used in the rest of the book.

PART I

Cultural Activities and Institutions

Primitive Beginnings

AT THE time of the Prophet Muḥammad no organized system of education existed in Arabia. The Bedouin boys learned from their fathers how to tend the camels, to care for the tents and to engage in raiding, while the boys of the oases mastered the art of date culture. As the girls married in their early teens, whatever they learned was from their mothers.

Although some of the Christians and Jews,[1] as well as the scribes and a few of the more progressive people of the towns, knew how to read and write, most of the Arabs were illiterate. Literary culture, however, was not entirely lacking, as there was a taste for proverbs and poetry[2] recited orally. The sons of the nomads spent hours in the black tents, listening to their elders recite tribal ballads, and one of the features of an annual fair,[3] held near Makkah, was a contest between the popular poets. In spite of this interest in verse, there were many dialects instead of a common language, and the old scripts were too inaccurate to make it possible to write anything other than treaties, contracts and formal communications.

In the midst of this primitive culture, Muḥammad's call to prophethood was like the planting of a seed, destined to blossom as the intellectual heritage of Islām.

Although the traditions[4] telling how the revelations became

1. There were Christians on the Byzantine frontier and also at Tabūk and Najrān. Jews were in al-Yathrib, Tabūk, Khaybar and other places. See Balādhurī, al-, *The Origins of the Islamic State,* trans. Phillip K. Ḥittī (Columbia Univ. Press, 1916), Part II, pp. 270-274; Nadīm, ibn-al-, *Kitāb al-Fihrist,* edit., Gustav Flügel (Leipzig, 1871), p. 5, line 18; Lammens, H., *Calife Omaiyade Mo'āwia ler* (Harrassowitz 1908), pp. 217, 218; Guillaume, Alfred, *Life of Muhammad* (Oxford Univ. Press, 1955) pp. 14, 79, 239, 510, etc.

2. The early verse included oracles, the *rajaz* or primitive rhyme and the *qaṣīdah,* with its praise of love and war.

3. Sūq 'Ukāẓ.

4. Bell, Richard, *Introduction to the Qur'ān* (Edinburgh Univ. Press, 1953) pp. 38-42; Nadīm, pp. 25-28.

codified may not be reliable, it is reasonable to believe that the Muslims, who were able to read and write, compiled one authorized version of the Qur'ān about a quarter of a century after the Prophet's death. This achievement provided the Muslim community with one official language and a generally accepted form of writing, which was improved as the scribes developed new scripts.[5]

For the early generations of Muslims this authorized version of the Qur'ān served as a basis of belief, worship, law and behavior. From the point of view of literary style, it was for the Muslims what the Iliad was for the Greeks. In connection with the law, it was what the Pentateuch was for the Hebrews. As a collection of inerrant revelations, it meant all that the Bible did for the founders of the Protestant movement.

Thus the Qur'ān was the foundation stone of Muslim education. We cannot understand Islamic culture, unless we realize that it did not deal with things devised by men, but rather with truths revealed by God. In fact subjects unrelated to the Qur'ān were regarded as being too secular to teach to the children. Muslim education was Qur'ānic education.

There is an Arab saying that "Knowledge and fire are the only two things which grow by being spread."[6] In the spirit of this proverb the Caliphs encouraged pious men to teach the Qur'ān in the mosques, so as to spread knowledge and increase learning.

In the course of time different types of teachers appeared. There was, for instance, the Qur'ān reader,[7] who explained the revelations to groups in the mosques. There was the popular moral teacher or story teller,[8] who illustrated his discourses with tales from the Qur'ān, similar to the ones in the Old Testament, and with accounts of the heroes of early Islām. There was also the relator,[9] able to quote Muslim traditions, Bedouin poems, elegies and proverbs, as well as anecdotes about the Prophet and his Companions.

Another kind of teacher was the tutor.[10] When the illiterate

5. Nadīm, pp. 7, 8.

6. Tritton, A. S., *Materials on Muslim Education in the Middle Ages,* (Luzac, 1957).

7. *Al-qurrā' or al-qārī,* who was inevitably a commentator.

8. *Al-qāṣṣ;* in modern Arabic *al-qaṣṣāṣ.* See Mez, Adam, *The Renaissance of Islam,* trans. Bakhsh & Margoliouth (Luzac, 1937) pp. 326, 344.

9. *Al-rāwī.*

10. *Al-mu'addib.* Before the Arabs themselves became educated, members of the conquered peoples served as tutors.

Arabs conquered the kingdoms of the Middle East, the spoils of war made their leaders so rich that they were obliged to train their children to manage large estates. When, moreover, they left their tents to live in ancient cities and new garrison towns, they had the additional problem of fitting their sons for urban life. Accordingly, they engaged private teachers to give lessons to their boys. The tutor was expected to offer all of the material used by the Qur'ān reader, story teller and relator of anecdotes and traditions, as well as simple arithmetic and the art of polite conversation. His pupils also learned horsemanship, swimming and the use of weapons.

This interest in educating both needy pupils in the mosques and rich boys in their homes encouraged enterprising teachers to start little schools, which were especially necessary for the children of foreign converts, unacquainted with Arabic. Although to begin with the teachers merely helped the children to repeat the Qur'ān parrot fashion, it was not long before they also taught their pupils to read and write, enabling them to study the meaning of the verses as well as to memorize the words. It was these humble beginnings which marked the first step in the development of Muslim education.

The Elementary School

By the middle of the eighth century a popular system of elementary school education became generally adopted. Although the classes were sometimes held in a shop or private house, they were much more often attached to a mosque. Between the ages of six and ten the children had little choice of subjects. The pupil copied a passage of the Qur'ān on his tablet. Then, after memorizing the first passage, he erased it so as to deal with a second one, continuing this process until the Qur'ān was completed. He also joined with his schoolmates in repeating the verses in a sing-song way, so as to keep from forgetting them. It was not uncommon for a boy ten years old to be paraded through the streets of the town as a reward for memorizing the entire Qur'ān.

The pupil also used proverbs and verses of poetry as models for his penmanship and as a rule was taught something about numbers and reckoning. Some time, moreover, before he reached the age of adolescence he was obliged to learn the rules for ritualistic ablution, the words and movements of prayer and the essential ordinances of Islām.

When a boy was at least ten years old and had completed the elementary school course, he was eligible to spend three additional years studying supplementary subjects. These included some vocabulary and penmanship, grammar, rhetoric and literature, as well as the history of the period in which the Prophet lived.

One old book[11] recorded that during the 'Abbāsid period the children used to have reading half the morning and, except for some recreation, writing the remainder of the day, the exercises being based upon the Qur'ān. On Tuesday afternoons and Thursday mornings the boys corrected what they had written. Friday was a day of rest and there were also holidays for the feasts. The tuition fee paid to the teacher, either monthly or annually, was determined by the court judges.

Whipping was used both for punishment and to teach the boys to be brave. One author, however, explains that the teacher should try to reason with a child before beating him and that, even if he did use corporal punishment, he should be careful not to injure a boy.[12] Another book says that beating was on the soles of the feet, three strokes of a whip or strap for a small boy and five to ten for an older one.[13] We may, however, be sure that many teachers had bamboo rods ready for use, not always being gentle when the pupils misbehaved.

In theory the teacher was supposed to be a well educated married man, neither too old nor too young. In a school of some importance he could choose a special subject such as the Arabic language, the Qur'ān, or the arithmetic required for applying the laws of inheritance. Because of dealing with religious subjects, the elementary school teacher was originally much respected, but he lost his prestige as the lower schools became overshadowed by higher education.

Although the early teachers felt it to be a pious duty to teach free of charge, it was not long before the school masters came to expect gifts of food and money, sometimes even allowing their

11. *Ādāb al-Mu'allimīn* of ibn-Saḥnūn, see Ṭalas, Asad, *La Madrasa Nizamiyya et son Histoire* (Geuthner, 1939) p. 10.

12. *Islām al-Yawm wa Ghadan* (Dar Iḥyā' al-Kutub al-'Arabīyah, 1957) pp. 58, 59. Ṭawṭaḥ, Khalil A., *The Contribution of the Arabs to Education* (Columbia Univ., 1926) p. 63. Shalabī, Aḥmad, *History of Muslim Education* (Dār al-Kashshāf, Beirut, 1954) p. 150.

13. Tritton *(Muslim Educ.)* p. 18. See also Ahwānī, Aḥmad, *Al-Tarbiyah fī al-Islām* (Dār Iḥyā' al-Kutub al-'Arabīyah, 1955) p. 146.

work to become commercialized. At the end of the Umayyad period, for instance, one school was said to have had three thousand pupils, the master riding from one class to another on a donkey.[14]

The teacher was accustomed to sit on a small stool, with thirty or forty pupils squatting on the ground around him. As slate was not easy to procure, the child wrote on a board, which could be scraped and washed in preparation for the next lesson.

Vocational Training

After completing the elementary school classes most of the boys worked with their fathers on the farms, or helped master craftsmen in the towns. The vocational education of medieval times consisted of the apprentice system, conducted in the small workshops of the bazaars.

A bazaar was a network of narrow streets, wide enough for a loaded donkey to pass through and often covered with wooden roofing, matting or strips of cloth.[15] On both sides of the alleys there were vaulted rooms, often not more than eight or ten feet wide, in which the artisans manufactured and sold their wares. These workers were organized in craft guilds, each with its own shaykh, who handled government relations and taxes, cared for the poor and sick, organized festivals, fixed the wages of the workmen, standardized forms of craft manufacture and determined the prices of goods. Each guild occupied its own quarter of the bazaar, so that the carpenters, blacksmiths, coppersmiths, rope makers, cloth weavers, goldsmiths, leather workers and other craftsmen worked side by side with members of their own trades. As the homes of the workers were as a rule outside of the bazaar, the shops were closed at night with wooden doors, while the quarters of the bazaar itself were protected by iron gates.

The master of a shop often had several assistants or journeymen, who in turn had apprentices to help them. These apprentices were apt to be boys who had completed some elementary school work and were the sons of the craftsmen in their shop, or of members of the guild to which their master belonged. As in medieval Europe, the apprentice learned his trade by practical

14. Tritton *(Muslim Educ.)* p. 1.

15. In Arabic a bazaar is called *al-sūq*.

experience, in due time becoming a journeyman, perhaps even the master of a craft shop. Not all of the apprentices worked in the crowded sections of the city, as some of them were attached to trades carried on outside of the bazaars, such as oil pressing, charcoal burning, soap making, stone cutting, brick manufacture and work in the lime kilns.

The system had its advantages as it provided the boys with free manual education, as well as with excellent discipline and a knowledge of human nature. By painstaking imitation the apprentices mastered the techniques of their elders, thus becoming some of the most skillful artisans who have ever lived.

On the other hand, the system had its faults because the forms of articles, wages, rents and prices were standardized by the guilds, preventing competition, individual initiative and industrial enterprise.

As a rule vocational training for the girls was limited to work in their homes, where their mothers taught them how to cook and keep house in preparation for early marriage. Only exceptional girls went to school or studied with private teachers.

There was, however, one class of girls who received a specialized training. In days gone by a poor child did not expect to become a Hollywood heroine, but the most enterprising among the children of poor families did have ambitions to succeed as palace favorites, perhaps as the mothers of high officials or even of caliphs. Many of the most famous rulers of Islām were the sons of concubines. Accordingly, a girl was not loath to become a slave in the hands of a dealer, who trained her so as to sell her for a good price. She learned how to dance and sing, how to chant the Qur'ān and the ancient poetry with musical taste and grammatical accuracy, and how to join in conversation about learned matters. If, in addition to her training, the girl had the sex appeal of a modern film star, she might become the concubine of a ruler, living in fabulous luxury and wielding great influence. Shajar al-Durr, for instance, was a foreign slave girl, who took the place of the Sulṭān of Egypt for a number of months, during the year 1250 A.D.

The famous vizier, Yaḥyā al-Barmakī, had a handmaid who was able to compete with scholars and poets in their own fields of achievement. The Caliph al-Wāthiq[16] also possessed a concubine of outstanding ability, trained by one of the great gram-

16. Yaḥyā al-Barmakī served as the vizier of Hārūn al-Rashīd. Al-Wāthiq was the 'Abbāsid Caliph, 842-847.

marians of al-Baṣrah.[17] One time she recited a verse containing the word "man," which she placed in the accusative. Although the Caliph himself thought that the girl was correct, some of the scholars of his court claimed that she was mistaken and that the word should be in the nominative. To settle the dispute the Caliph had the grammarian brought all the way from al-Baṣrah on the Persian Gulf to his palace city of Sāmarrā, south of ancient Nineveh. When the grammarian gave his verdict that the word should be in the accusative, in accordance with the opinion of the Caliph and the rendering of the concubine, al-Wāthiq gave the grammarian five thousand silver coins, sending him back to his home with high honors. As a rule this training given to the concubines was of a specialized and vocational nature, so that higher education inevitably developed among the boys, rather than the girls.

Advanced Study

As Muslim society became increasingly complex, many of the boys desired to fit themselves for successful careers by studying courses more advanced than those of the elementary school. One authority classified these ambitious students in the following way. In the first place, there was the type of boy who aspired to become a mosque leader,[18] or the teacher of some specialized subject. In the second place, there was the student enjoying study for his own personal satisfaction. Thirdly, there were ambitious youths desiring social prestige and, finally, there were the boys who wished to earn a living by means of intellectual training.[19]

Because there were no secondary schools, a boy seeking higher learning was obliged to study with an independent teacher, whose classes were of an informal nature, usually conducted in a mosque. During the Middle Ages there were three principal types of classes.

In the first place, there were lectures attended by large groups of students. As a rule the teacher sat on a low chair, leaning against a column and facing Makkah, while he dictated to the

17. Abū 'Uthmān Bakr ibn-Muḥammad al-Māzinī. See Nadīm, p. 57; Yāqūt, *Irshād al-Arīb ilā Ma'rifat, al-Adīb, edit.* D. S. Margoliouth (Luzac, 1907 ff.); Khallikān, *Ibn Khallikan's Biographical Dictionary,* trans. M. de Slane (Paris, 1843). The story is also told by al-Zubaydī *(Ṭabaqāt al-Naḥwīyīn wa'l Lughawīyīn,* p. 92), and al-Suyūṭī *(Bughyat al-Wu'āt,* p. 202). See also, *Enc. of Islam,* Vol. IV, p. 702, "Tawaddud".

18. *Al-imām.*

19. *Islamic Culture,* Oct. 1944, pp. 419-422.

students with the help of his assistants. The students were accustomed to sit on straw mats spread out on the paved floor, forming an irregular semicircle. Even if a scholar of this type was popular enough to have several hundred members of his class, he encouraged questions and discussion after he had finished dictating his material.

The second type of class was a circle,[20] which was small enough to allow the teacher to explain his subject in an intimate way and to encourage lively discussion, while the students took down notes and asked questions. If the teacher was a good man, he took a fatherly interest in the moral and social life of his pupils, so that the personal nature of this form of instruction made it an especially valuable method of education. The teacher might meet his pupils in a mosque or in his home, but always in an atmosphere of intimacy and sympathetic understanding.

The third type of instruction may be described as discipleship. A boy[21] lived with a scholar long enough to acquire most of his master's learning. Sometimes the pupil was well-to-do, paying for the privilege of studying with the scholar, while at other times the boy was a slave, who by copying manuscripts and helping his master with his work became a scholar himself. More often the pupil was a poor boy, who performed domestic duties and copied manuscripts in return for the opportunity of associating with his patron and the learned men frequenting his master's house. It was not unusual for a boy of this sort to feel closer to his employer than he did to his own father, even calling himself by his master's name. Thus an apprentice of the great scholar of al-Baṣrah, Ibn-Durayd, called himself "al-Duraydī." One reason why these pupils were so well trained was because their masters were strict disciplinarians. Once, for instance, a pupil of a learned scholar made a grammatical error in a public place. The master scolded him saying, "By Allāh, if I were at home I'd beat you, but the people here will not stand for that."[22]

A student might spend most of his life with one scholar, sometimes marrying his daughter and becoming his successor, or he might study with numerous teachers, learning language from one, the Qur'ān from another and additional subjects from other

20. The Arabic word *al-ḥalaqah* was used both for the small circle and large class.

21. The word *al-ghulām* was used for a boy of this type, as well as for boys of other kinds.

22. Nadīm, pp. 61-62.

masters. Usually a student did not devote himself to more than one subject at a time, but al-Nawawī, who died in 1278, attended twelve classes.

In connection with all of these different types of instruction, the students often helped their teachers to compile books, writing down what was dictated, comparing their various notes, discussing their material and making numerous corrections. Finally, when the work was approved by the teacher, the material was copied with good penmanship, so as to form a handwritten volume. Abū-Bakr ibn Durayd composed

> the book *al-Jamharah* about the science of language. It had diversities in its transcribing, with many additions and cancellations, for he dictated some of it in Persia and some from memory at Baghdād. When the dictation was inconsistent, he added and subtracted. The part which he dictated to his pupils in Persia was the beginning of the book, whereas the complete form, regarded as reliable, is the last transcription. The person who finally transcribed the material . . . wrote it from a number of manuscripts after reading it over with the author.[23]

Pedagogy was the subject of numerous articles, one of which was composed by al-Zarnūjī in 1203 A.D. A few of his sayings are worth recording, as they clearly reveal the medieval point of view. "Stick to ancient things while avoiding new things." "Beware of becoming engrossed in those disputes which come about after one has cut loose from the ancient authorities." "The best periods (for study) are at the beginning of adolescence as well as the hour of dawn and that between the setting of the sun and the first vigil of the night." "The most forceful factors in (strengthening) memory are industriousness and assiduousness." (Also) "A reduction of eating as well as praying at night and reading the Koran are among the causes of remembering." Al-Zarnūjī also explained that a student should memorize as much as possible each day by repeating a passage twice, or if possible ten times. Then he should add new passages day after day, always repeating the things already learned.[24] These principles emphasize the importance of piety, ascetic living and memory training as requisites for advanced study.

23. *Ibid.*, p. 61.

24. Zarnūjī, al-, *Ta'līm al-Muta'allim—Ṭarīq at-Ta'allum,* trans., von Grunebaum & Abel (King's Crown Press, 1947) pp. 28, 58, 67, 46.

In some places there were public discussions in the streets as well as in the mosques. Thus at the market place of al-Baṣrah[25] the language scholars mingled with the Bedouin traders, so as to learn their dialects. At the same time poets held contests and heated arguments.

Another center for training the youth was the government chancellery,[26] where after completing the elementary school course a boy could learn the art of writing official communications. Many sons of officials profited by this training, some of them becoming the ablest masters of Arabic style in medieval times.

One of the most eminent thinkers of the early period was al-Jāḥiẓ,[27] whose experiences are very revealing. After memorizing the Qur'ān at an elementary school he frequented the mosques of al-Baṣrah, so as to learn as much as possible from the language students, dictionary compilers, reciters of poetry and relators of the traditions. Instead of limiting his interests to one study circle, he attended as many classes as he could and in addition spent long hours in the market place, studying Bedouin expressions. While earning his living by doing the marketing for a famous scholar,[28] he devoted twenty-four years to learning the Islamic sciences and an even longer period to studying the translations of Greek books. As he was the most brilliant scholar of his time, he was an exception, the normal boy being satisfied to learn one subject at a time.

In connection with this medieval education there are five points to bear in mind, a number of which have already been mentioned. In the first place, education was not institutionalized. The pupil was obliged to be his own dean and registrar. As there were no entrance requirements or examinations and certificates did not come into use before the first part of the tenth century, there were no true academic standards. In the second place, there was apt to be an intimate relationship between the teacher and his students, which was one of the best features of Muslim education. The third point is that memory was all important. The mature student memorized the notes which his teacher dictated to him, just as the child learned the Qur'ān. A few illustrations explain what extraordinary memories this system produced.

25. *Al-Mirbaḍ*, see Pellat, Charles, *Le Milieu Baṣrien et la Formation de Ǧāḥiẓ* (Adrien-Maisonneuve, 1953) p. 11; Ṭalas, pp. 6, 7.

26. *Dīwān al-Inshā'*.

27. Pellat, Intr. p. xiv and pp. 63-69. Kahallikān, *(Biog. Dict.)* Vol. II, p. 405. Nadīm (Beatty MS.) p. 112.

28. Ibrāhīm ibn-Sayyār al-Naẓẓām, who died about 845 A.D.

Muḥammad ibn-Ziyād al-A'rābī of al-Kūfah, who died at Sāmarrā in 840 A.D., met with a hundred pupils. He dictated to them for ten years, during which time nobody ever saw a manuscript in his hand, as he had a prodigious memory.[29]

One ninth century author said, "Mu'arraj had a better memory than other people. He caught a passage from me and remembered it all night, repeating it the next day, although it was about fifty pages long."[30]

Another scholar went from Baghdād to Sijistān to give a course of lectures. In order to avoid carrying books, he memorized the traditions to which he wished to refer. The story was that although he quoted thirty thousand traditions about the Prophet, the persons checking his lectures were unable to find more than three mistakes.[31]

It is probable that anecdotes of this sort were exaggerated and that in spite of their excellent memories the medieval scholars did not always quote their sources in an accurate way. Thus the author of *al-Fihrist* rendered some lines of the great poet Jarīr differently from the way they have been preserved in an anthology of the poet's own compositions.[32]

A fourth point to bear in mind is that medieval education did not produce originality. Most of the scholars commented on what they learned from their masters, without trying to add new ideas of their own. Al-Rummānī, for instance, wrote ten books about the works of other authors, and eight books about pedantic questions, which did not require original ideas.[33] Even research was more concerned with gathering data than with forming new theories and introducing progressive methods.

Finally, the Muslim empire was so vast that scholarship was exceedingly cosmopolitan. The life of a scholar who was called the "Crown of Islām" illustrates this point very clearly. He visited Transoxiana and the cities of Khurāsān, as well as Qūmis, al-Rayy, Isfahān, Ḥamadhān and many centers in 'Irāq, Syria and the Ḥijāz, listening to lectures and gaining knowledge from a great

29. Khallikān *(Biog. Dict.)* Vol. III, p. 24; Nadīm, p. 69.

30. This was probably Mu'arraj ibn-'Amr ibn al-Ḥārith, a pupil of al-Khalīl ibn-Aḥmad, who died 810.

31. The scholar was 'Abdallāh ibn Sulaymān, see Mez, Adam, *The Renaissance of Islām,* trans. Bakhsh & Margoliouth (Luzac, 1937), p. 191.

32. Nadīm, p. 57; *Sharḥ Dīwān Jarīr,* edit., Muḥammad Ismā'īl al-Sāwī (Al-Sāwī Press, Cairo) pp. 304, 305.

33. Nadīm, p. 63. The pupil was usually said to "quote" his master, rather than to produce anything original of his own.

number of different authorities. During the eleventh century another scholar walked from Tabrīz in Persia to al-Ma'arrah in Syria, carrying his books in a bag, in order to consult the famous poet abū-al-'Alā' about some statements which he wished to have confirmed.[34]

Some anecdotes about an authority named al-Farrā'[35] throw further light on the methods of these medieval scholars. When a government official needed information about the ordinances of the Qur'ān, he asked al-Farrā' to supply him with facts in written form. Accordingly, al-Farrā' said to his companions, who were probably his pupils, "Come together so that I can dictate to you a book about the Qur'ān." "In the mosque there was a man who gave the call to prayer and read to the people during their devotions. Turning to him al-Farrā' said, 'Read the opening of the Book,[36] so that I can explain it.' Then they continued through the Book (Qur'ān) as a whole, the man reading and al-Farrā' explaining." After they had edited the explanations which were dictated to them, the pupils produced a work entitled *Ma'ānī al-Qur'ān*.[37]

The reason why al-Farrā' dictated his book called *al-Ḥudūd* was

> Because a number of the associates of al-Kisā'ī[38] came to him, asking him to dictate to them some information about grammar. He complied, but when they met for the third time some of them said to the others, 'As he keeps on teaching grammar for small boys, it's time to break away from him!' When they left him he grew angry saying, 'They asked me to meet and then when I came they absented themselves, but by Allāh I'll dictate the grammar even if only two turn up.' Thus he dictated his material for sixteen years, during which time no book was ever seen in his hand, except on one occasion when he dictated the chapter Mulāzim.[39]

The leading pupil of al-Farrā' was named Tha'lab. He must have passed his childhood at Baghdād, because when he was four

34. The scholars were abū-Sa'd 'Abd-al-Karīm al-Samānī (1074-1116) and al-Khaṭīb al-Tabrīzī, see Ṭawṭaḥ, pp. 8, 9.

35. A grammarian of al-Kūfah, who died about 822. See Nadīm, pp. 66, 67.

36. Al-Fātiḥah, the opening section of the Qur'ān.

37. Translations from Nadīm, pp. 66, 67.

38. A grammarian of al-Kūfah, who became tutor to the sons of Hārūn al-Rashīd. See Nadīm, p. 65.

39. Translated from Nadīm, pp. 66, 67. *Mulāzim* was the sixth chapter of *Kitāb al-Ḥudūd* entitled *Mulāzamat Rajul.*

years old his father held him on his shoulder to see the Caliph al-Ma'mūn ride by. He began his serious study when he was sixteen and by the time that he was twenty-five had memorized the books of al-Farrā', so that he could say "Not one of their letters escaped me." He also said "I was more concerned with grammar than with other subjects, but when I had mastered it I became intent on poetry, rhetoric and rare forms of expression."[40] After studying these different subjects and associating with an elder scholar[41] for ten years, he became so famous that students flocked to his classes. It is easy to picture him with his ample head covering and handsome beard, as he sat on a low chair with an eager group of students sitting around him on the ground. His leather slippers were beside him, his manuscript near at hand and his brass inkwell fixed in the broad girdle, which held in place his flowing robes.

As a rule the classes met between early dawn and the middle of the morning, at which time the students were given a chance to eat a combined breakfast and lunch. Classes were held also between the noon and afternoon prayers, after which there was a recess for study and supper. Many students liked to meet their teachers after the sunset prayer, during the cool of the evening. In the great mosque of Old Cairo a hundred and ten classes were accustomed to meet at this time to study the Qur'ān, legal subjects, literature and philosophy.[42] The student was free to choose the teacher, subject, class circle and hour that he desired. He also determined whether he should attend one class or numerous ones, the system being voluntary without compulsion or restraint.

This interest in advanced study developed a new social class in Islām. Although the scholars were not rich they must have been happy, as the old Arabic books contain many anecdotes about their sense of humor, amusing stories and practical jokes. They were also greatly honored because of their learning and impressive robes,[43] as well as their interest in training the youth.

40. Nadīm, p. 74. See also Khallikān *(Biog. Dict.)* Vol. I, p. 83.

41. Ibn-al-A'rābī who lived about 765-845. See Nadīm, p. 69.

42. Tritton *(Muslim Educ.)* pp. 61-65.

43. The Egyptian astronomer, 'Alī Yūnus, wound his turban around a high peaked cap, placing his head drapery over that. See Khallikān *(Biog. Dict.)* Vol. II, p. 365. The Fāṭimid scholar wore a *qalansuwah,* probably a sort of cap, and a *sabnī,* or girdle, with a black *taylasān dabsī,* or veil-like cape, over his head and shoulders. See Dozy, R., *Dictionnaire Détaillé des Noms des Vêtements Chez les Arabes* (Amsterdam, 1845) pp. 365, 200, 278; Shalabī, pp. 153, 154. In the course of time it became the custom for the rulers to confer robes of honor on the scholars, especially when they paid their respects for the Feast of Ramaḍān.

The Use of Paper

One of the most revolutionary events in the development of education was the manufacture of paper.[44] Parchment and papyrus were so difficult to procure, that it was a tremendous stimulus to learning when the Muslims acquired the art of paper making. This new industry started in Samarqand during the eighth century, when some Chinese prisoners taught the local artisans how to make paper out of flax and hemp cloth.

The manufacture of paper created a new profession, that of the *warrāq,* who dealt in paper and also copied manuscripts to sell to his customers. He spent most of his time in his own shop, which was perhaps a stall on the street level, or else a pleasant upper chamber removed from the dust of the bazaar.

If the *warrāq* was a learned man, he attracted other scholars to his shop, so that it became an informal club for academic discussion. Sometimes a *warrāq* like the author of *al-Fihrist*[45] was not content to copy and sell other men's compositions, but contributed original work of his own. Thus by serving as a copyist, stationer, book dealer and publisher, the *warrāq* played an important role in intellectual circles.

The medieval manuscripts were not in the form of scrolls, but of books with paper leaves, which were often held together by leather covers. Although these paper books were cheaper and easier to handle than the parchment ones of earlier times, they were too expensive for the ordinary student to buy. As, therefore, the teachers could not send their students to a college store to buy textbooks, they were obliged to waste valuable time dictating notes. Probably because there was a prejudice against duplicating the Qur'ān in a mechanical way, most of the Muslim communities did not have printing presses before the nineteenth century.

The transcribing of manuscripts by hand was, therefore, a very important form of occupation. Not only teachers and students, but also well known authors, copied books in order to earn money. *Kitāb al-Fihrist* frequently speaks of books copied in the handwriting of famous scholars. There are also references to men like al-Karmānī, whose calligraphy was "in demand."[46]

Some of the old records make it possible to compare the size

44. Compare Mez, pp. 467-469.

45. Abū-al-Faraj Muḥammad ibn-Isḥāq al-Warrāq known as ibn-abī-Ya'qūb al-Nadīm.

46. Nadīm, pp. 77, 79, 82, etc.

of a handwritten book with that of a modern printed volume. Thus it was stated that the famous *Kitāb al-Aghānī* filled five thousand leaves of a handwritten manuscript, whereas the modern printed edition fills five volumes, each with about four hundred pages, and one shorter volume with two hundred and eighty pages.[47]

In spite of the fact that many people transcribed manuscripts, the handwritten manuscripts were inevitably expensive, being limited in number. It was, accordingly, difficult for scholars in Baghdād to procure copies of books written in other places. In speaking about al-Hunā'ī, for instance, it is stated that "His writings can be obtained in Egypt, where they are sought after," making it evident that they could not easily be procured in 'Irāq.[48]

Because of the shortage of books, the high government officials established great libraries, while the schools and mosques made more modest collections of books and written documents. Some of the largest libraries were in Bayt al-Ḥikmah at Baghdād, the royal palace, Mosque of al-Azhar and Dār al-Ḥikmah in Fāṭimid Cairo, the great mosques of Fās in Morocco and the intellectual centers of Spain.[49]

Only a few of the individual scholars were rich enough to procure private libraries of importance. There were, however, a number who enjoyed government patronage and opportunities to collect books. Thus it is related that

> After his death al-Wāqidī left behind him six hundred cases of books, each case a load for two men. He had two young men slaves, who wrote for him night and day. There had also been sold to him books costing two thousand gold coins.[50]

Although there were librarians, it must have required patience to use the old books, as they were often clumsy to handle and the handwritten catalogues were inconvenient. It was also difficult to keep the books in good order, as the Islamic lands were dusty, with pests of insects, which devour paper.

The scholars, moreover, did not have the conveniences which we enjoy in modern times. They lacked good lighting at night, comfortable desks and private collections of books, as well as modern inventions such as fountain pens, typewriters, card

47. *Ibid.*, p. 115.
48. *Ibid.*, p. 83.
49. Compare Mez, pp. 172-177.
50. Nadīm, p. 98, line 25.

catalogues and many other things. It is therefore impressive to appreciate the extent of their achievements. The great medical authority abū Bakr Muḥammad al-Rāzī wrote a hundred and thirteen books and twenty-eight epistles or monographs, while the philosopher al-Kindī produced a hundred and thirty-seven books and sixty epistles.[51] Even though some of the books were more like long chapters than complete volumes, these medieval authorities must have been exceedingly industrious, whether they dictated their works to their students or wrote them down themselves with reed pens.

Translation and Research

The classes devoted to Qur'ānic and linguistic studies were supplemented by other forms of higher learning. During the last half of the eighth century the Caliph al-Manṣūr summoned a physician[52] to come from the famous medical center of Southern Persia to the court at Baghdād. This doctor and other scholars interested the Muslims in Greek science and philosophy.[53]

At the same time a great Sanskrit work on astronomy was translated into Arabic, the astrolabe was introduced as a scientific instrument and the Indian system of numerals was brought to Baghdād.[54]

The Caliph Hārūn al-Rashīd, a contemporary of Charlemagne, not only encouraged the study of foreign sciences, but also established a hospital[55] at Baghdād. In 830 his son, the Caliph al-Ma'mūn, went a step further by founding at Baghdād a research institute, known as "Bayt al-Ḥikmah," or the "House of Wisdom." This institution was more like the Museum of the Ptolemies in Alexandria than a modern university. It comprised an astronomical observatory, a translation bureau and a great library, serving research scholars and their disciples rather than large numbers of immature students. It was especially important be-

51. *Ibid.*, pp. 299-302 and 255-260.

52. Because of persecution and exile, the medical authorities of the Graeco-Roman world sought refuge in Persia, where they established a medical center at Jundīshāpūr. About 756 A.D. the Caliph brought the Nestorian Jūrjīs ibn-Bakhtishu' to Baghdād, where his son further developed his work. Nadīm, p. 296.

53. See Nadīm, p. 243 ff.; Ḥittī, Phillip K., *History of the Arabs* (Macmillan, 1949) pp. 306-316, 363-387; Sarton, George, *Introduction to the History of Science* (Carnegie Inst. of Washington, 1927) Vol. I; O'Leary, de Lacy, *How Greek Science Passed to the Arabs* (Routledge & Kegan Paul, 1949) the entire book.

54. Muḥammad al-Fazārī was chiefly responsible for these services.

55. Al-Bīmāristān.

cause it formed a basis for collecting foreign manuscripts and translating scientific books. In the course of time Plato, Aristotle, Hippocrates, Galen, Ptolemy and many other ancient authorities became known, their works being translated accurately enough to enable hundreds of Arabic speaking scholars to study them.

Valuable research was undertaken, especially in connection with astronomy, medicine and pharmacy, while Greek logic and philosophy inevitably influenced the development of Muslim theology. Private philanthropists, like the banū-Mūsā at Baghdād and ibn-Sawwār at al-Baṣrah, patronized research, while the caliphs and high government officials held cultural meetings in their palaces and gave generous presents to encourage scholarship.[56]

It was not long before Egypt also became a center of scientific studies. Before the end of the ninth century ibn-Ṭūlūn built a hospital at Cairo and in 988 a Fāṭimid Caliph provided funds to organize higher education at the Mosque of al-Azhar, where at least for a number of years philosophy and astronomy were taught, in addition to the linguistic and Qur'ānic studies.[57]

At the same time the Fāṭimid rulers made large collections of manuscripts and encouraged lectures in what they called the Court of Science[58] in their palace. In 1005 the Caliph al-Ḥākim founded an institute for research and advanced study. It was called *Dār al-Ḥikmah,* or the Court of Wisdom, and like its rival institution at Baghdād contained an important library. Scholars coming from many parts of the Muslim world were provided with paper, ink and pens, so that they could work in the comfortable rooms set apart for them, the women being assigned apartments of their own. Some of the scholars came to read, some to transcribe manuscripts and others for research. As there were special sections for the different academic subjects, with professors to give free lectures, the institution was an important center of learning. Unfortunately, however, it did not exist for more than a short period of time and its atmosphere was colored by the peculiar ideology of the Fāṭimids. Al-Ḥākim also built an observatory on the hills back of Cairo, employing famous scholars[59] to conduct astronomical research.

56. For bānī-Mūsā, Nadīm, p. 271; for *Dār al-Kutub* of ibn-Sawwār, Pellat, p. 66. The lectures were *al-majālis.* See also, Ṭawṭaḥ, pp. 6, 7.

57. Ḥusayn, Muḥammad Kāmil, *Dīwān al-Mu'ayyad fī al-Dīn* (Dār al-Kātib al-Miṣrī, 1949) p. 57, note 2.

58. *Dār al-'Ilm.*

59. The best known were 'Alī ibn-Yūnus and al-Ḥasan ibn-Haytham.

A medieval encyclopaedia[60] gives the names of so many learned men, who translated ancient texts and wrote books of their own during the first four centuries of Islām, that one can appreciate the importance of this scientific movement. During the four centuries which followed, other scholars further developed Muslim science and philosophy, not only in Egypt, but also in North Africa, Spain, Syria, Persia and Afghanistān.

Because of the downfall of the Fātimids, the Crusades, the Mongolian invasions, the Christian conquest of Spain and the expansion of the Ottoman Empire, only a few enterprising spirits kept alive an interest in secular subjects. War, tyranny and exploitation made life so painful that most of the scholars shrank from the affairs of this world, seeking admission to paradise by means of religious studies, ascetic living and mysticism.

Thus, although the scientific movement greatly enriched the intellectual life of Islām, it did not influence medieval Muslim education in a permanent way. Instead of being generally accepted as legitimate subjects of the curriculum, science and philosophy were taught by special teachers, frequently in their own homes instead of in the mosques.

Government Aid

During a period when rulers were despotic and the common people illiterate, it is not surprising that the cultural life of medieval Islām depended to a great extent upon government support. Except for the ascetics and mystics, who composed religious verses as a pious duty and lived in extreme simplicity, most of the poets depended upon the gifts of government officers and wealthy patrons for their livelihood.

Some of the scholars earned enough to live on by teaching, copying manuscripts and taking part in commercial enterprises. A larger number, however, enjoyed government aid in one form or another. They served as judicial authorities, court companions, palace tutors and the secretaries of official bureaus. Al-Kisā'ī, for instance, was tutor to the sons of Hārūn al-Rashīd and abū-al-'Amaythal taught the children of 'Abdallāh ibn-Ṭāhir, the viceroy in Khurāsān.[61] The tenth century grammarian, al-Fārisī, was so handsomely cared for at the courts, first of Sayf al-Dawlah at Aleppo and later of 'Aḍud al-Dawlah in Shīrāz, that his life and

60. *Kitāb al-Fihrist,* see Nadīm in the bibliography.
61. Khallikān *(Biog. Dict.)* Vol. II, pp. 123 and 55.

work were exceedingly brilliant. On the other hand, another scholar known as al-Akhfash al-Aṣghar was so unsuccessful in obtaining the support of his local vizier, that he died about 927 A.D. from undernourishment.[62]

Famous medical authorities like abū-Bakr Muḥammad al-Rāzī and ibn-Sīnā[63] were liberally supported by generous rulers, because of their gift of healing. Many scholars were granted livings in research institutions like the Bayt al-Ḥikmah in Baghdād and Dār al-Ḥikmah in Cairo, supported by government grants. Other men of learning were given large contributions in payment for writing books for individual rulers. Thus abū-Isḥāq al-Zajjāj wrote a commentary for the Caliph al-Mu'taḍid, which won him an enviable position at court and an allowance of three hundred gold coins.[64]

During the eleventh century and the period which followed, the high government officials not only aided individual scholars, but also gave generous grants to support colleges, dervisheries, libraries and other institutions like hospitals, orphanages and mosques. These government endowments and assignments enabled large numbers of scholars to teach, study and compose books. Not only the great sulṭāns but also scores of less important officials established these charitable and educational institutions, making it possible for Muslim culture to flourish throughout the Middle Ages. From the point of view of education, the most important of these philanthropies were the colleges and mosque-colleges.

The College

It proved to be so inconvenient to hold lectures and lively discussions in the mosques, where pious worshippers were trying to pray and to memorize the Qur'ān, that the Muslim educators developed a new type of institution called in Arabic "al-madrasah," referred to in English as the "college." This form of school did not bring to an end the educational work in the mosques, but existed side by side with the mosque classes.

Although the term "al-madrasah" was used during the ninth century, the first institution really deserving the name was probably built at Naysābūr in North-Eastern Persia during the first

62. *Ibid.*, Vol. I, p. 379; II, p. 244.

63. *Ibid.*, Vol. III, p. 311, Vol. I, p. 440. In Europe they were known as Rhazes and Avicenna.

64. Nadīm, p. 60.

quarter of the eleventh century.[65] Then in 1067 Niẓām al-Mulk[66] erected at Baghdād the great college, which became a model for orthodox Islām and was named after its founder "al-Niẓāmīyah," the Caliph himself presiding over its dedication.

The building was a quadrangle located near the Tigris, probably with colonnades or half open vaulted halls surrounding a central courtyard. On the side facing Makkah there was undoubtedly a prayer niche, with a pulpit standing near it, and somewhere in the building there was a library of considerable importance. Either on upper floors or in adjoining loggias there must have been sleeping quarters for the students, while in the basements there were store rooms, lavatories and a kitchen. Most of the classes probably met in the porches or colonnades, although it is possible that there were a number of individual classrooms. As the building was completely destroyed, it is impossible to know exactly what it was like.[67]

The teacher followed the old custom of sitting on a low chair, with his students on the ground around him. When a lecture was given, it began with prayer, followed by the recital of some verses from the Qur'ān and an appeal for Allāh to bless the Prophet.

Niẓām al-Mulk provided large enough endowments to assure generous salaries for the teachers as well as board, lodging, clothing, furnishings and heat for the students. The professors, who wore academic robes of black and marine blue, were so highly regarded that they were frequently chosen to perform diplomatic missions. Whenever a professor gave his first lecture it attracted many important persons, who attended a banquet as soon as the class was ended.

The honorary head of the college was a high official, with a deputy or vice-chancellor to conduct the administration. As a rule each professor had at least one assistant and in addition to the members of the teaching staff there were numerous clerks and servants as well as the librarian, prayer leader and registrar.[68]

65. Suyūṭī, al-, *Ḥusn al-Muḥāḍarah fī Akhbār Miṣr wa'l-Qāhirah* (al-Mawsū'āt Press, Cairo) Part II, p. 156.

66. When the Saljūq Turks gained control of the 'Abbāsid Caliphate, Niẓām al-Mulk became their famous vizier. The college was built to combat revolutionary Shī'ite propaganda. Every teacher was expected to subscribe to the legal system of al-Shāfi'ī and the theology of al-Ash'arī.

67. See Ṭalas, entire book, for a description of al-Niẓāmīyah.

68. The deputy was *al-nā'ib,* the professor *al-ustādh* or *al-mudarris,* the deputy professor *nā'ib al-tadrīs,* the assistant *al-mu'īd* and the registrar *kātib al-ghaybah.* The student was *al-ṭālib,* sometimes honored with the title of *al-faqīh.* In Ayyūbī and Mamlūk times an administrator or professor entitled to use a chair was *al-shaykh,* a beginning pupil *al-mubtadī,* the student starting to specialize *al-mufīd* and a postgraduate student *al-muntahī.*

The assistant repeated the words of the professor in a loud voice, so that the students could write them down from dictation. He also answered questions, explained the lessons and helped the students to correct their notes. In case an assistant took the place of an absent professor, he showed proper respect by holding his master's manuscript in his hand and praying for his safe return.

After removing his shoes a student sat on the ground, often using his knees to serve as a desk. He held his paper in his left hand, while with his right hand he wrote from right to left, dipping his reed pen in an inkstand, which was as a rule a small brass container inserted in a wooden pen box fixed to his girdle. The notes, which the student took down from dictation and memorized, served as his textbook.

There was no regular schedule, the student being free to continue his studies as long as he himself and his teachers felt it wise for him to do so. Time was not an important factor, the principal aim of the system being thoroughness. The professor started his course by giving an outline of the material to be studied, followed by a general explanation of the subject and the ways in which the authorities differed about it. Finally there was an exhaustive study of every aspect of the material. In order to avoid confusion the student was advised to study one subject at a time and to refrain from using too many sources. He was also encouraged to learn logic and rhetoric, so as to know how to avoid ambiguity of language and thought. As, however, the bright students were too ambitious to limit their efforts to studying only one course at a time, it was not long before it became the custom for them to study a number of subjects every day.

Most of the teachers were true scholars and men of good character, sincerely interested in their students. Many of them were known for their piety, frugality, industry, kindness and sense of humor. They had, however, certain shortcomings, one of which was the tendency to imitate rather than to create. They were also accused of being vain and envious. Competition to have large classes, jealousy at time of failure and self-satisfaction when there was success, were frailties which gave a human touch to these men of religion and learning.

The famous traveller ibn-Jubayr visited al-Niẓāmīyah about 1184 and was much impressed by a lecture, which he attended one Friday afternoon. The gathering must have been of a special nature, as classes did not as a rule meet on Fridays. After several reciters had intoned passages of the Qur'ān, a religious leader delivered an address from the top step of the pulpit, commenting on the Qur'ān and the traditions of the Prophet. After he had finished his discourse, questions in written form were showered on him from all sides. He answered them in a patient way, throwing away the paper on which each question was written, after the answer had been given.[69]

Niẓām al-Mulk established colleges like al-Niẓāmīyah at al-Baṣrah and al-Mawṣil in 'Irāq, at Iṣfahān and Naysābūr in Persia, and Balkh and Harāt further to the east.

A century later, Saladin[70] founded five colleges in Cairo, to take the place of the heretical classes, which had existed there during the Fāṭimid régime. As the members of his dynasty added twenty-six other colleges and the Mamlūk Sulṭāns added many more, there were forty-five colleges in the older parts of Cairo and seventy in the newer quarter of al-Qāhirah during the first half of the fifteenth century.[71]

One building still standing is the Madrasah of Sulṭān Ḥasan, which was built in 1359 to serve as a college, but subsequently was turned into a mosque. On the outside it looks like a huge cube, with stone walls three stories high, beautified by a magnificent archway over the main entrance. Corridors lead to the central courtyard, which is square with a fountain in the middle. On each one of the four sides there is a large vaulted hall, or "līwān," entirely open in the direction of the courtyard. In the four corners of the building there are accommodations for the four orthodox legal codes. These apartments provided living quarters for the students and a few small classrooms. Each code was also allowed to use a "līwān" for lecture courses and religious exercises.

Although this great college and a number of others of similar importance served all four codes of the law, most of the institutions attempted to teach only one or two of the legal codes. Some

69. Jubayr, ibn-, *The Travels of ibn-Jubayr,* trans. R. J. C. Broadhurst (Jonathan Cape, 1952) pp. 228, 238; also edit., M. J. de Goeje (Librarie Orientale, Paris, 1907), p. 219.

70. The Sulṭān Ṣalāḥ-al-Dīn Yūsuf ibn-Ayyūb.

71. In 1171 Saladin built al-Nāṣirīyah and soon afterwards al-Qamḥīyah and al-Suyūfīyah in Old Cairo, al-Ṣalāḥīyah near the tomb of al-Shāfi'ī, and a fifth college at the shrine of al-Ḥusayn in al-Qāhirah. The most important colleges founded by his successors were al-Kāmilīyah, established by the Sulṭān al-Kāmil, and al-Ṣāliḥīyah built by the Sulṭān al-Ṣāliḥ Ayyūb. The Mamlūk Sulṭān Qalāwūn and his sons and the Sulṭān Ḥasan erected colleges which were especially famous. See Suyūṭī, Part II, pp. 156, 157, 160; Khallikān *(Biog. Dict.)* Vol. III, pp. 241, 242; Vol. IV, p. 547; Maqrīzī, al-, *Kitāb al-Khiṭaṭ al Maqrīzīyah* (al-Nīl Press 1906) Part II, p. 340; Part IV, pp. 192, 193, 196, 209, 211, 221. For the development of college architecture see Creswell, K. A. C., *The Muslim Architecture of Egypt* (Clarendon Press, 1952-1959) Vol. II, pp. 104-134, 195-198, 234-248, 253.

of the colleges were small with one or two classrooms, while others were extensive with lecture halls and student cells placed around spacious gardens.[72]

By the end of the fourteenth century there were ten colleges in North Africa,[73] while many others existed on the other side of the Muslim world in Persia, Afghanistān and Central Asia. Many beautiful institutions were also founded in India after the Muslim invasion. One student of education[74] has estimated that in medieval times there were 73 colleges in Damascus, 41 in Jerusalem, 40 in Baghdād, 14 at Aleppo, 13 in Tripoli, 9 in al-Mawṣil and 74 in Cairo, in addition to numerous institutions in other cities.

The college which at this period most closely resembled a university was founded at Baghdād in 1234 and called "al-Mustanṣirīyah." It was built on the shore of the Tigris as a large two storied structure, oblong in shape with a great open court in the center. Around the courtyard there were rooms for teachers and students, opening out to arched cloisters.

At one end of the building there were four lecture halls for the four codes of law. Each one of them probably had a prayer niche, so that it could be used for devotions as well as for classes. Somewhere in the building there were store rooms, a large library, a kitchen and bathing facilities. Attached to the college there was a hospital with a dispensary and rooms for teaching medicine. One of the curiosities of the institution was a famous clock, set in a design of the heavens, with twelve doors opening to announce the hours. As royal endowments supported the college, the students received food, medical care and financial aid, in addition to free tuition.

For each one of the four codes of law there were sixty-two students, taught by a head professor and his assistants. The curriculum not only included the traditional linguistic, legal and religious subjects, but also arithmetic and the division of inheritance, land surveying, history, poetry, hygiene, the care of animals and plants and other phases of natural history. There was also a course in medicine with a physician in charge.

72. Al-Nāṣirīyah built in Cairo in 1296 provided for all four codes, whereas the colleges of Ṭaybars and Āqbughā adjoining the Mosque of al-Azhar are examples of smaller ones. Numerous institutions established in Persia and India at a later period were built around handsome courtyards.

73. Ziyādah (N. A. Ziadeh), *Sanūsīyah* (E. J. Brill, 1958) p. 5; *Enc. of Islam* (Brill & Luzac, 1913) Vol. III, pp. 381-388.

74. Ṭawṭaḥ, p. 23.

When a professor gave a lecture he sat on a chair under a dome, dressed in black, with an assistant on each side to dictate to the students. In addition to the lectures there must have been more intimate classes, as it is recorded that one teacher of the traditions taught only ten students, Mondays, Thursdays and Saturdays. Each code of law had its own prayer leader and in the library there was a librarian with an assistant and attendants. In an annex of the college there were thirty orphan boys studying the Qur'ān. Although al-Mustanṣirīyah was not destroyed when the Mongolians sacked Baghdād, it fell to pieces during the Ottoman period, so that it is no longer used for educational purposes.[75]

The Dervish Monastery

In medieval times one of the important members of Muslim society was the Ṣūfī, who devoted himself to ascetic practices and mysticism. It was not long before groups of ascetics organized brotherhoods and founded monasteries,[76] to provide homes for the members of their orders. Because study of the Qur'ān was regarded as a valuable means of attaining sanctity, these institutions did a great deal to encourage education.

Some of the large fraternities organized classes of their own, while others provided living accommodations for their members, who were studying in other institutions. Even today the dervish orders are serving as educational centers in places where other schools are lacking.[77]

So many of the Ṣūfī scholars became teachers in the mosques and colleges, that Muslim education was permeated with the doctrines of mysticism. Progress gave way to fatalism, scientific study to superstition and academic initiative to imitation. Thus, at the same time that the monastic movement encouraged education, it helped to produce intellectual stagnation.

The Mosque-College

Even after the college had become a popular form of education, the old mosques continued to serve as seats of higher learning. There was still a lack of system, as teen-age boys and white

75. Creswell *(Egypt)* Vol. II, pp. 124-127; Maqrīzī *(Sulūk)* Vol. I, p. 312. Ṭalas, pp. 44, 53-55. Ma'rūf, Nājī, *al-Madrasah al-Mustanṣirīyah* (Nādī al-Muthannā, Baghdād, 1935) entire pamphlet.

76. The monastery or dervishery was called *al-ribāṭ, al-khānaqāh* or *al-zāwiyah*: plural *al-rubūṭ, al-khawāniq* or *al-zawāyā*.

77. Ziyādah, pp. 106, 114.

haired men studied in the same buildings, with no provision for entrance requirements, prescribed courses or examinations. Holidays were long, textbooks difficult to procure and memory work all important. There was, moreover, no income from tuition charges, because instead of paying fees most of the students received bread or other forms of aid.

As in the past, there was no provision for staff appointments. A young man, who gained the respect of his professors, was allowed to establish himself as a teacher by forming a circle of his own in the mosque building. If he failed, he moved to a less important mosque, but if he succeeded, his position was confirmed by the assignment of a fixed place for his classes and perhaps a small honorarium in the form of money or bread. There was really no clear cut distinction between the faculty and student body, as an ambitious young man often taught one subject at the same time that he was studying another one.

In at least three ways, however, the old mosque system was affected by the educational developments of the period. In the first place, a new system of certificates became generally accepted. The certificate[78] was not conferred by the institution, but was granted in a personal way by an individual professor, stating that his student had completed the material of his course so as to be able to teach it. The document was written by hand on an unofficial piece of paper, with long pious phrases praising the student, sometimes in an exaggerated way. In fact the professor often wrote a lengthy testimonial, more concerned with literary style than with an honest appraisal of the student's ability. After a student had been able to collect certificates from a number of teachers, he was in a position to seek employment in a mosque, college, law court, government office or village school.

In the second place, the mosque was influenced by the medieval tendency to standardize the content of the courses, so that the same subjects were taught throughout the Muslim world. Originality and experiment were regarded as dangerous, whereas imitation and orthodoxy were upheld.

In the third place, the more important mosques competed with the colleges by providing residential quarters for students who did not have nearby homes. The principal mosques in the large cities, which are often referred to as "mosque-colleges," became such important centers of higher learning that a number

78. *Al-ijāzah.* For an example, see Dodge *(Al-Azhar)*, p. 198.

of them are still in existence, whereas most of the ancient colleges have disappeared.

There were mosque-colleges in many of the provincial towns, but the most important ones were in the capital cities, where they were endowed by the rulers. Although the studies in all of these institutions were conducted in a similar manner, there were different ways of providing for the boarding pupils.

In the Mosque of al-Azhar at Cairo, for instance, each student was assigned to a residential unit for the sake of registration and discipline.[79] The unit was endowed so as to care for the boys from some Egyptian province, foreign country or legal system. The mosque was built around an open courtyard, with the sanctuary in the rear and spacious cloisters or loggias on both sides of the court. Doors and stairways led from these loggias to rear rooms, upper chambers and basements. Each unit occupied a section of these residential quarters, providing living space for students who did not have homes in Cairo. A large residential unit often included a library, kitchen and lavatory, in addition to space for the chests in which the students stored their belongings. There was also a common lavatory for general use.

These living quarters were so cluttered with storage chests that, except in winter weather, the boys preferred to sleep and study in the open courtyard, rather than in the crowded loggias and inner rooms. A student was often so poor that he borrowed straw matting from the sanctuary to take the place of a mattress, using his long robe as a blanket. As a rule his residential unit gave him free bread, while his family often supplied him with other forms of food to cook on a small brazier. Some of the students, however, were able to afford to live in lodgings near the mosque, with sufficient food and clothing to be comparatively comfortable.

As a student prayed five times a day and his first class began before sunrise, his life was not very different from that of a monk in a European monastery. It is no wonder that the system at al-Azhar was an old-fashioned one, the first living quarters having been built there in 988 A.D.[80]

The accommodations in many of the mosque-colleges, which were built during a later period in Irān, Pakistān and other

79. The large unit was *al-riwāq*. In medieval times there were probably about two dozen of these units. The small space was *al-ḥārah*. Thirteen of these small units were still in existence during the early twentieth century.

80. For a more detailed account of al-Azhar, see Dodge, B., *Al-Azhar, a Millennium of Muslim Learning* (Middle East Inst., 1961) chap. I-IV and Appendix III.

regions, were often more comfortable, with student rooms surrounding central gardens. At Fās in Morocco and al-Najaf in 'Irāq another method for providing for the students was used. This plan is of special interest, because it is so similar to the system adopted by Oxford and Cambridge.

Until very recently the great Qarawīyīn was a mosque-college, with classes supported by endowments and an academic atmosphere similar to that of the other medieval institutions. It was founded at Fās[81] during the middle of the ninth century and, after serving for a time as one of the three or four schools of the city, became the principal center of higher learning in Morocco. The boarding students of the Qarawīyīn did not live in the mosque, but in residential quadrangles, each one of which was called a "madrasah" or college. These quadrangles contained two and three story buildings ranging in size from accommodations for sixty to a hundred and fifty students.

The students' cells opened out to porches surrounding the large open courtyard of the quadrangle. Each student received drinking water, one loaf of bread a day and the use of a cell. As he had to buy the right to occupy his room and was obliged to tip the guardian[82] of the quadrangle, he was apt to share a cell with one or two friends. This room in the quadrangle was used for study, sleeping, cooking and recreation, whereas the classes were as a rule held at the mosque.[83]

The best place in the world to study the atmosphere of a medieval mosque-college is al-Najaf in 'Irāq, a short distance to the west of ancient Babylon. It is an especially sacred place for the Shī'ite branch of Islām as it contains the tomb of 'Alī, the Prophet's son-in-law. Because of its sanctity, Shī'ite rulers and philanthropists have established endowments and are constantly making new contributions, to support the mosques of the city, as well as the residence halls associated with them. About half of the scholars are married, living in their own homes, but the others are accommodated in twenty-four quadrangles similar to those at Fās.

Although one quadrangle has a second story, each of the others

81. Fās in Morocco. The mosque became very important before the end of the sixteenth century.

82. *Al-muqaddam.*

83. There were six colleges still in existence at the end of the Second World War. For al-Qarawīyīn see Le Tourneau, Roger, *Fès Avant le Protectorat* (Société Marocaine de Librarie et d'Edition, Casablanca, 1947), pp. 453-471; Coon, Carleton, *Caravan* (Henry Holt, 1951) pp. 254-258; *Enc. of Islam* (1913) Vol. II, p. 76. *Muslim World,* 1958, Vol. XLVIII, pp. 104-112, "The Karaouine at Fez," by Rom Landau.

has only a main floor, built over a basement, which rises a meter above the ground. These quadrangles, like the ones at Fās, are called "colleges," some of which maintain classes as well as living quarters.

If you enter one of these quadrangles, you will come upon a spacious open courtyard, beautified by a central pool of water. On all four sides of the court there are pleasant rooms, with large doorways to give light and ventilation. A jar of drinking water is sure to be hanging in the wind to cool, the water in the pool being used for washing and ablutions. Inside the room you will find a young scholar clad in Oriental garb, seated on the floor with some paper, ink and cheap publications by his side and a textbook on a small rack in front of him. In one corner you will find a small oil stove, a basket of provisions and some loaves of bread. Unless changes have been made during the past year or two, you will see no table, chair, wardrobe or bedstead in the student's room, but instead a box to hold clothing, some inexpensive bedding, a piece of straw matting and perhaps also a rug on the floor.[84]

Some of the students receive aid from their colleges, while others are supported by their families, by giving lessons, or by serving in the mosques of the town. As in the medieval centers, the students range in age from teen-age boys to men of maturity.[85]

A number of the leading centers of Muslim education were in Spain, but they ceased to function when the Muslims were driven from that country. In other lands, however, mosque-colleges continue to exist without radical changes. One of the best known among them is al-Zaytūnah, which was built in Tunisia in 732 A.D. and still exerts a great influence.

Not only in the Arab lands, but also in Turkey, Irān, Pakistān and India, there are magnificent buildings, which once served as centers of learning. Education and religion were so closely bound together that during medieval times these great mosque-colleges were institutions of national importance.

The aim of the educators in the colleges and mosque-colleges was not to make discoveries or to seek the truth by means of research and experiment. The scientific method was regarded as dangerous, whereas it was felt to be a pious duty to memorize

84. Description based upon the observations of the author, when he visited al-Najaf.

85. See the important article by Fāḍil Jamālī in *The Muslim World,* January, 1960, pp. 15-22.

ancient texts, subscribing to the orthodox doctrines. The principal purpose of this medieval education was to teach the students to accept the truths, revealed to the Prophet and interpreted by the forefathers. It was inevitable, therefore, for the curriculum to be devoted to the language of the Qur'ān, the laws revealed by Allāh and the religious tenets of Islām. The following list gives the principal subjects, which formed the program of studies throughout the Middle Ages.

The Medieval Curriculum

A. The Revealed Sciences and Sciences of the Arabic Language.[86]

The Arabic Language	*al-lughah*
Grammar	*al-naḥw*
Rhetoric	*al-balāghah*
Literature	*al-adab*
Readings (Qur'ānic)	*al-qirā'āt*
Exegesis (Commentary)	*al-tafsīr*
Traditions (of the Prophet)	*al-ḥadīth*
Law	*al-fiqh*
Sources or Principles of the Law	*uṣūl al-fiqh*
Theology	*al-tawḥīd, al-kalām* or *uṣūl al-dīn*

B. The Rational Sciences.[87]

Mathematics	*al-riyāḍiyāt*
Division of Inheritance	*al-farā'iḍ*
Logic	*al-manṭiq*

The Rational Sciences were regarded as supplementary to the other studies. As a rule mathematics was taught in connection with the fixing of the times of prayer, fasting and religious feasts, or else with the division of inheritance. Logic was included, because ever since the time of the theologian al-Ash'arī it was regarded as useful for the defense of orthodox doctrines.

Many individual scholars studied philosophy, astrology, astronomy, geometry, medicine, pharmacy and certain aspects of the natural sciences, as well as alchemy, but these subjects were as a rule taught by private teachers in their homes or else in the hospitals. The basic curriculum of medieval times did not include

86. Al-'Ulūm al-Naqlīyah wa-'Ulūm al-Lisān al-'Arabī.
87. Al-'Ulūm al-'Aqlīyah.

secular subjects, but was devoted to studies explaining the revelations of the Qur'ān and their application to everyday life.

In order to know what the intellectual atmosphere of medieval Islām was like, it is necessary to be acquainted with these subjects. It is also true that one cannot appreciate the modern renaissance of Islām without a knowledge of these traditional studies, which formed a background for the courses of our own time.

Accordingly, the second part of this book is devoted to the basic subjects of the medieval curriculum and the way in which they developed, so as to become important elements in Muslim education.

PART II

Development of the Subjects of the Curriculum

The Arabic Language

THE ORIGINAL purpose of Muslim education was to explain the divine revelation and, because the Qur'ān was revealed in Arabic, the first step was to understand the Arabic language. No man could be a successful government official or judge, a lawyer, mosque leader or teacher, unless he was familiar with Arabic.

At the time of the Prophet the Arabic language was very imperfect, as it was a medley of tribal dialects with a primitive form of script. Although Muḥammad himself employed scribes to write his official documents, they did not attempt to compile a written version of the entire Qur'ān. These scribes probably lacked both parchment and papyrus, being obliged to use a form of red leather as writing material.

A few of the Prophet's relatives and Companions knew how to write well enough to inscribe some of the verses of the Qur'ān on palm stems, white stones and pieces of bone, but as long as Muḥammad lived they too failed to compile the Qur'ān as a whole. Thus during the life time of the Prophet, except perhaps for some tribal poetry, written Arabic was not sufficiently developed to be used for literary purposes.[1]

When, however, Muḥammad himself and many of his intimate associates, who had memorized verses of the Qur'ān, came to the end of their lives, it was essential to preserve all of the divine revelations in written form. Accordingly, during the last half

1. For references about writing during the Prophet's time see Nadīm, p. 5, line 18. Lammens *(Mo'āwia)* pp. 217, 218; Ṭabarī, al-, *(Annales)*, edit. M. J. de Geoje (Brill, 1883-1884) Part I, p. 1782; Balādhurī, Part I, pp. 92, 93; Part II, pp. 84, 270-274; Guillaume *(Life of Muhammad)* pp. 643-646, 649, 653-658; Khaldūn, ibn-, *(Muqaddimat ibn-Khaldūn)*, edit., M. Quatremère (Benjamin Duprat, Paris, 1858) Part II, p. 339; *(The Muqaddimah)*, trans., Franz Rosenthal (Bollingen Series xliii, Pantheon Books, 1958) Vol. II, pp. 377, 378.

of the seventh century an authorized version of the Qur'ān was compiled for use by the Muslim community as a whole.[2] This step gave the Arabic language definite form, but it was only the beginning rather than the culmination of language study.

Although the official version was composed in the vernacular of the Quraysh Tribe to which Muḥammad belonged, the colloquialisms of other tribes found their way into the sacred book, making it difficult to understand. No single Arab was familiar with all of the words, while the foreign converts were as a rule unable to read the simplest passages.

Furthermore, the Kūfic script, in which the authorized version was written, was awkward to read and full of ambiguities.[3] Not only were the letters difficult to identify, but they also lacked the supplementary signs, which give definiteness to well developed Arabic writing. Many of the Arabic consonants have identical forms, except as they are distinguished by dots, placed above and below the line. Double letters are also indicated by a small sign, while vowels are designated by little marks rather than by separate letters.

As even a number of new scripts invented by the scribes[4] lacked these supplementary signs, the writing continued for many years to be indefinite and the language imperfect. Eventually, however, consonant and vowel signs were adopted[5] and such intensive research was carried on in connection with the colloquialisms in the Qur'ān, that the science of "al-lughah," or language, came to be formed.

In speaking about philology or the analytical study of the language, Dr. George Sarton has written, "The discovery of the logical structure of language was as much a scientific discovery as, for example, the discovery of the anatomical structure of the body." "The scientific study of language was considerably stimulated in mediaeval times by the religious necessity to interpret sacred writings which were supposed to be infallible."[6] These words very definitely apply to Arabic and the Qur'ān.

Ibn-Khaldūn also emphasized the importance of linguistic studies when he said that "A knowledge of them is absolutely necessary for the jurists, because the articles of the law are

2. Nadīm, pp. 25-28; Bell, pp. 38-42; Ḥittī *(Arabs)* p. 123.
3. Khaldūn (Quatremère) Part II, p. 342; (Rosenthal) Vol. II, p. 382.
4. Nadīm, pp. 7, 8.
5. Pellat, p. 76; Ḥittī *(Arabs)* p. 219; Bell, p. 43; *Enc. of Islam* (1913) Vol. I, p. 381.
6. Sarton, Vol. I, p. 7.

derived from the Qur'ān and the sunnah,[7] which are in the Arabic language."[8]

There were two especially important centers for this language study, both of which were garrison towns built by the Muslims when they conquered 'Irāq. One of them was al-Kūfah, a few miles south of the ruins of Babylon, the other being al-Baṣrah at the head of the Persian Gulf. These settlements became centers of language study, because they were frequented by foreign converts seeking to learn Arabic, as well as by nomads using the tribal dialects of Arabia.[9]

Pious scholars spent years of their lives in collecting Bedouin terms and idioms connected with camels, horses, palm trees, hunting, water sources and other things, their purpose being to learn the meaning of the strange words in the Qur'ān. One scholar, for instance, compiled a large work called *Kitāb al-Ṣifāt,* described by an ancient authority in the following way. "The first section deals with the character of man, liberality, generosity and also the qualities of women. The second section deals with tents, houses, descriptions of mountains and ravines, as well as merchandise. The third section is devoted to the camel. The fourth section deals with flying clouds, the sun and moon, night and day, milk, mushrooms, wells, cisterns, well ropes, buckets and a description of wine. The fifth section discusses planting, vines, grapes, the names of herbs, trees, winds, clouds and rain." This same author wrote shorter books about the horse, weapons, the stars, divisions of water on desert expeditions, and vernacular expressions in tribal legends.[10]

Thus the language scholars studied Bedouin anthropology, in order to understand the strange expressions appearing in traditions about the Prophet, and in the Qur'ān itself. They memorized the tribal poems and studied nomadic lore, writing books and developing their studies into a science. One great scholar named al-Aṣma'ī[11] made an extensive collection of the poems which he studied and abū-'Ubaydah[12] wrote nearly two hundred books about

7. The sayings and precedents of the Prophet.

8. Khaldūn (Quatremère) Part III, p. 279; (Rosenthal) Vol. III, p. 139.

9. See Ḥittī *(Arabs)* p. 241. For the scholars attached to these centers see Nadīm, pp. 39-77.

10. The author was al-Naḍr ibn Shumayl, who died about 819 A.D. Nadīm, p. 52.

11. He died at al-Baṣrah between 828 and 832. See Nadīm, p. 55; Khallikān *(Biog. Dict.)* Vol. II, p. 123.

12. He lived from 733 to 825. See Nadīm, p. 53; Khallikān *(Biog. Dict.)* Vol. III, p. 388.

tribal folklore and the Arabic language. Yūnus ibn-Ḥabīb of al-Baṣrah was so keen about collecting vernacular expressions that it was said about him, "Yūnus lived for eighty-eight years. He did not marry or have a concubine, his only interest being study and conversation with men."[13]

A very important contribution to this language study was made by al-Khalīl[14] when he compiled the first Arabic dictionary. It was named for the Arabic letter *al-'ayn,* which represented the first sound emitted by the organ of speech. In the course of time dictionaries became so common that ibn-Khaldūn recorded that they were to be found in Spain, North Africa, Persia and other places. He mentioned in particular a lexicon called *Fiqh al-Lughah,* written by al-Tha'ālibī.[15] He also said that "Abridgments for this department of study, especially for words in general use, are very numerous. They have been composed to make it easy for the students to learn by heart the meaning of the terms."[16]

By means of these dictionaries and linguistic studies, the scholars made it possible for their students to understand the rare forms and colloquialisms in the Qur'ān and the traditions of the Prophet. They also evolved a great literary language, which throughout the Middle Ages was the rival of Latin.

In the course of time this language study was rendered more precise by the development of grammar, which included "al-naḥw" or syntax, and "al-ṣarf," with its analysis of conjugation, declension and other things. It is probable that foreign converts helped to form this subject of the curriculum, as they were familiar with the grammatical systems used by the Greeks, Hebrews and other ancient peoples.

Grammar

According to an ancient tradition, a scholar of al-Baṣrah[17] devised Arabic grammar when he found that ignorance of case endings was leading to a false interpretation of the Qur'ān. Two of the earliest books about the subject were composed by a blind

13. He died about 799. See Nadīm, p. 42.
14. Al-Khalīl ibn-Aḥmad of al-Baṣrah lived about 712-786. See Khallikān *(Biog. Dict.)* Vol. I, p. 493. For dictionary compilers, see Nadīm, pp. 42, 43, 72, 74; Mez, pp. 236, 237.
15. A scholar of Naysābūr, 961-1038 A.D., famous for his anthology.
16. Khaldūn (Quatremère) Part III, p. 288; (Rosenthal) Vol. III, pp. 328, 329.
17. Abū-al-Aswad al-Du'alī, see Nadīm, p. 39; Ḥittī *(Arabs)* pp. 241, 242.

scholar who died about 767,[18] but the great textbook was written by Sībawayh, a Persian scholar living in 'Irāq at the time of Hārūn al-Rashīd. His work entitled "al-Kitāb," or "The Book," summed up the rules of grammar so perfectly that a later scholar was able to say, "if anybody wants to write an important book about grammar in addition to "al-Kitāb" of Sībawayh, he ought to be ashamed of himself."[19]

The first scholar of al-Kūfah who wrote about grammar was called al-Ru'āsī, or "Heady," because of his enormous head. His most famous pupil was nicknamed al-Kisā'ī on account of his *kisā'* or cloak.[20] So many other grammarians are mentioned in the second chapter of *Kitāb al-Fihrist* that one can appreciate how important grammar came to be as one of the Muslim sciences.[21]

The medieval grammarians wrote books about spelling, pronunciation, correction of speech, the singular, dual and plural numbers, gender, consonant and vowel signs, agreements and disagreements, starts and stops, long and short *alifs*, the weak letters and other technicalities. Grammar explains the conjugation of the verb and the use of different verbal forms, each with its own significance. It also gives the rules for indicating the cases, like nominative, genitive and accusative, as well as for the proper use of the subject and predicate. It deals, moreover, with adjectives, prepositions and other forms.

This science of grammar was considered to be so essential both for understanding the Qur'ān and for writing Arabic correctly, that as late as the nineteenth century a student was expected to master a different textbook every year or two for at least ten years, most of the books being studied twice over with different teachers.

Even this painstaking study, however, did not satisfy the Muslim scholars. In order to interpret the expressions in the Qur'ān with still greater accuracy and to encourage exact diction in writing and preaching, they developed another subject called in English rhetoric and in Arabic the science of "al-balāghah" or "al-bayān."

18. 'Isā ibn-'Umar al-Thaqafī. See Nadīm, p. 41.

19. 'Amr ibn-'Uthmān Sībawayh died 793. See Nadīm, p. 51, 52 line 1; Khallikān *(Biog. Dict.)* Vol. II, p. 396.

20. Abū-Ja'far Muḥammad al-Ru'asī and abū-al-Ḥasan 'Alī al-Kisā'ī. See Nadīm, pp. 64, 65.

21. See Nadīm, pp. 39-88; Khaldūn (Quatremère) Part III, pp. 279-283; (Rosenthal) Vol. III, pp. 323, 324. Also *Tabaqāt al-Naḥwīyīn wa'l-Lughawīyīn* by al-Zubaydī (al-Khanjī Press, Cairo, 1954) and *Bughyat al-Wu'āt* by al-Suyūṭī (Al-Sa'ādah Press, Cairo, 1909).

Rhetoric

The old processes of composition and prosody used by the poets led to the development of rhetoric. The purpose of the study is contained in a quotation from abū-Hilāl al-'Askarī: "When composing poetry and writing essays a student of Arabic can, by means of al-balāghah, differentiate between desirable and undesirable words, and phraseology in either good or objectionable style."[22]

As the science of rhetoric developed it was divided into three main branches. The first of these, *al-ma'ānī,* is concerned with clear expression and the use of different kinds of sentences. It depends upon grammar for its methods and gives a knowledge of the forms of phraseology, making it possible to avoid errors and to express the desired meaning.

The second branch, *al-bayān,* teaches the art of expressing ideas with eloquence and without ambiguity. It tries to make the meaning entirely accurate, giving the sole interpretation intended. In connection with good literary style it also deals with simile, metaphor and nomenclature.

The third branch of rhetoric, *al-badī',* is concerned with the perfection of the wording and embellishment of speech. It teaches the student how to make one phrase suit another, avoiding mixed figures of expression. It also takes into account the relationship between the final words in a line of poetry and those preceding them.

Ibn-Khaldūn explains the kind of problems dealt with by rhetoric when in discussing the use of emphasis he gives three examples concerning a man named Zayd. "Zayd is standing;" "Truly Zayd is standing;" "Truly it is Zayd who is standing." Then he adds that each one of these phrases must be analyzed, so as to arrive at its true meaning. He also gives another illustration when he cites the metaphor, "Zayd is a lion" and explains that rhetoric accurately interprets the significance of the metaphor.[23]

As rhetoric is not merely theoretical, but also has practical value for preachers and authors, it has always been an important subject, still being taught in modern times. Although rhetoric, grammar and other forms of language study are dry, technical subjects, they form a basis for the far more interesting "science of al-adab" or literature, composed of "belles-lettres" and poetry.

22. Free translation from *Dā'irat al-Ma'ārif,* Vol. IV, pp. 65-72.
23. Khaldūn (Quatremère) Part III, pp. 290, 291; (Rosenthal) Vol. III, pp. 321-323.

Literature

Long before the time of the Prophet Muḥammad the nomads of Arabia composed beautiful verses, poetry being the music of the desert. Prose, on the other hand, did not take the form of good literature for many generations.[24] The early Muslims were occupied too much with their political, legal and religious problems to use prose for other than practical purposes.

One of the pioneers of prose literature was the famous scholar al-Jāḥiẓ, who wrote literary articles and entertaining stories in addition to more serious books. In describing his efforts to study literature he said,

> I sought knowledge of poetry from al-Aṣma'ī, only to find that his work was nothing more than a study of strange forms. Then I went to al-Akhfash and discovered that he did not go thoroughly into anything except his grammatical terms. In fact I only came across what I wanted with the men of letters among the government secretaries.[25]

As these secretaries handled the official correspondence of the caliph and his high officials, they prided themselves on their literary style. Instead of spending their time studying religious subjects, they devoted themselves to elegant composition. Many of them compiled anthologies of their epistles in book form, their letters often resembling modern essays. One authority has said about these letters that they were "The finest production of Muslim art."[26]

In addition to the ornate compositions of these secretaries, there were also popular works of great literary value. *Kalīlah wa-Dimnah*[27] was a collection of animal fables from India, translated into Arabic during the first half of the eighth century. There was also *Kitāb al-Aghānī,*[28] a huge compendium of poetic and prose passages, with many stories about the caliphs, poets, singing girls and popular heroes. There were, moreover, numerous collections of tales like *Alf Laylah wa-Laylah* or the *Arabian Nights,* which

24. Ḥittī *(Arabs),* pp. 402-405. Nicholson, R. A., *A Literary History of the Arabs* (T. Fisher Unwin, 1923), pp. 31, 346-348. Von Grunebaum, G. E., *Medieval Islam* (Univ. of Chicago Press, 1953) pp. 250-257. For sources of *al-adab* see Khaldūn (Quatremère) Part III, p. 296; (Rosenthal) Vol. III, pp. 340, 341.

25. Free translation from *Dā'irat al-Ma'ārif,* Vol. IV, p. 65. For authors named see Nadīm, pp. 55, 83, 53. For the compositions of the secretaries, see Qalqashandī, Vol. I and II; Nadīm, pp. 115-140.

26. Mez, p. 242.

27. The translator was ibn-al-Muqaffa', see Khallikān *(Biog. Dict.)* Vol. I, p. 431.

28. Compiled by abū-al-Faraj al-Iṣbahānī, 897-967.

had considerable literary value and helped to make prose popular.[29]

In speaking about literature the "Muqaddimah" states that "The mainstays of this science are four collections, namely 'Adab al-Kātib' of ibn-Qutaybah, 'Kitāb al-Kāmil' of al-Mubarrad, 'Kitāb al-Bayān wa'l-Tabyīn' of al-Jāḥiẓ, and 'Kitāb al-Nawādir' of abū-'Alī al-Qālī al-Baghdādī."[30]

Belles-lettres reached their culmination during the tenth and eleventh centuries. An author of Persian origin invented a new type of literature about the exploits of a hero, as he encountered many experiences. It was called "al-Maqāmah,"[31] which was a dramatic type of story telling, "A romance of literary Bohemianism," striking, because of its originality and masterful use of the Arabic language. This form of writing was further developed by al-Ḥarīrī, who wrote his "Maqāmāt" about the adventures of a hero named abū-Zayd.[32] The stories are of a popular nature, but the highly ornate diction, expressed both in poetry and prose, makes the work a masterpiece of literary style.

Although prose came to be respected as a beautiful form of literature, the truest expression of Arab genius was in the form of poetry. In spite of the fact that he disliked pagan verse, the Prophet Muḥammad encouraged his associate Ḥassān ibn-Thābit[33] to compose poetry for the Muslim community. After the Prophet's death, poetry became more and more popular, as first the Umayyad Caliphs of Damacus and later the 'Abbāsids at Baghdād favored their court poets.

As has already been explained, the language scholars collected Bedouin poems, in order to study the colloquialisms and tribal terms appearing in the Qur'ān. This study led to the formation of anthologies,[34] which preserved the old poems, making it possible for literary men to enjoy them.

29. See Nadīm, p. 304; von Grunebaum, p. 294 ff.

30. Khaldūn (Quatremère) Part III, p. 296; (Rosenthal) Vol. III, p. 340. For the authors mentioned see Nicholson *(Lit. Hist.)* pp. 343, 345, 420.

31. The author was Badī' al-Zamān al-Hamadhānī, 969-1008. The quotation is from Nicholson *(Lit. Hist.)* p. 328.

32. The author was abū-Muḥammad al-Qāsim al-Ḥarīrī of al-Baṣrah, 1054-1122. See Khallikān *(Biog. Dict.)* Vol. II, pp. 490, 493.

33. For samples of his poetry see Guillaume *(Life of Muhammad)* pp. 345-349, 430-433, 478-481, 488-489, 537-539, 795.

34. Some of the best known collections of poetry are:

(i) *al-Mu'allaqāt,* primitive odes probably edited during the 8th century and regarded as masterpieces.

(ii) *al-Mufaḍḍalīyāt,* an anthology of 128 early poems collected by al-

The high government officials encouraged poetry for two entirely different reasons. The first one was of a practical nature. It was so easy for the people to memorize and pass on popular verses expressing their political feelings, that poetry served as the principal medium of publicity. It was therefore necessary for the rulers to bribe the poets to refrain from satire and to be profuse with flattery. When the caliphs lavished gifts on their court poets, it was often with the same motives which lead modern rulers to subsidize newspapers.

A second reason why the caliphs and governors patronized the poets was because poetry became one of their principal forms of diversion. In former times, when there were few amusements and even the best lamps gave inadequate lighting at night, poetry served as a means of relaxation. This was especially true in the palaces, where the verses were often sung by the beautiful girls of the harem. The boon companion of Hārūn al-Rashīd,[35] for instance, made the ballads popular, because he was a great musician, expert in training slave girls.

Poems were not only popular in the palaces, but also in the resorts of the lower classes, where entertainers told stories and repeated verses. Thus poetry became as much sought after in the gathering places of the cities as in the black tents of the desert.

The Arabic poems contained praise of patrons, satire for both friends and foes, philosophical contemplation, elegies for the dead, songs of the chase and especially glorification of wine and women. The leading poets were just as greatly honored by the Arabs as Virgil, Horace and Ovid were by the Romans. A book written at the end of the tenth century[36] gives the names of so many persons who composed poetry, that it is impossible to mention all of the medieval poets. A few examples must suffice to illustrate what poetry stood for as one of the literary studies of the curriculum.

Four especially popular men lived while the Umayyad Caliphs

Mufaḍḍal al-Ḍabbī, who died about 786.

(iii) *al-Ḥamāsah,* compiled by abū-Tammān Ḥabīb ibn-Aws, who died about 850.

(iv) *al-Ḥamāsah* of al-Buḥturī, 820-897.

(v) *Kitāb al-Aghānī* of abū-al-Faraj al-Iṣbahānī, 897-967.

(vi) *Yatīmat al-Dahr* of abū-Manṣūr al-Tha'ālibī of Naysābūr, who died about 1037.

For a brief account of the anthologies, see Nicholson *(Lit. Hist.)* pp. 128-131, 348.

35. Isḥāq ibn-Ibrāhīm al-Mawṣilī, 767-850, see Nadīm, p. 140.

36. *Kitāb al-Fihrist,* see Nadīm, maqālah IV.

were ruling at Damascus.[37] 'Umar ibn-abī-Rabī'ah, the son of a merchant of Makkah and a brilliant composer of licentious verse, died in 719, famous for the love affairs which inspired his poetry. One of his companions, al-Akhṭal, lived from about 640 to 710 and, although he was a Christian wearing a cross in the presence of the caliph, he championed the divine right of the Umayyads to rule the Islamic state. Skilled in both flattery and satire, he was especially famous for his verses about sex and the cup.

There were two younger competitors of al-Akhṭal. One of them was al-Farazdaq, who, after being expelled from al-Baṣrah because of his satires, found favor at Damascus where he served as the court poet of four caliphs. Although he was a dissolute character and praised the descendants of 'Alī hostile to the Umayyads, the caliphs were willing to overlook his licentious living and political heresy on account of the beauty of his poetry. There was also Jarīr ibn-'Aṭīyah, whose poetry had great propaganda value, because he was a master of satire and extravagant praise. He died about 729 during the last great reign of the Umayyad Dynasty.

Two poets of the early 'Abbāsid period also became very famous.[38] One of them was abū-Nuwās, equally well known for his bad morals and good verse. He lived until about 810, being pictured in the *Arabian Nights* as the playmate of the Caliph Hārūn al-Rashīd. Many critics believe that his poetry was the finest lyric and Bacchic verse in Arabic literature.

His contemporary, abū-al-'Atāhiyah, was the member of a Bedouin tribe, who, while selling pottery at Baghdād, was shocked by the extravagance and dissoluteness of the capital. Although the caliph lavished money on him, he lived like an ascetic, writing about religious and philosophical subjects instead of liquor and love. His poetry is full of pessimism, based on the frailty of man and the vanity of worldly pleasures.

There were also two very great poets, belonging to a later generation and living in the provinces instead of at Baghdād. Al-Mutanabbī[39] was born at al-Kūfah in 915 and, after serving

37. For these poets see Iṣbahānī, al-, *Kitāb al-Aghānī* (Dār al-Ṭibā'ah, Cairo, 1868) Part I, p. 30; VII, p. 38, 169; IX, p. 2; X, p. 2. Khallikān *(Biog. Dict.)* Vol. II, p. 372; III, p. 612; I, p. 294. Ḥittī *(Arabs)* pp. 250-252. Nicholson *(Lit. Hist.)* pp. 237-245. As translation destroys the music of this type of poetry, it does not seem to be worthwhile to give examples in English.

38. See Iṣbahānī, Part XVIII, p. 2; III, p. 126. Khallikān *(Biog. Dict.)* Vol. I, pp. 391, 202. Nicholson *(Lit. Hist.)* pp. 292-303.

39. Abū-al-Ṭayyib Aḥmad ibn-Ḥasan called al-Mutanabbī. See Khallikān *(Biog. Dict.)* Vol. I, p. 102.

Sayf-al-Dawlah at Aleppo, he became the protégé of Kāfūr, who ruled Egypt shortly before the Fāṭimid invasion. He later visited Persia and in 965, during the course of his travels, was killed by bandits. Although his style may be too ornate to suit the Anglo-Saxon taste, many Muslim authorities regard his poetry as having pre-eminent importance. One critic said about him, "He moulds the most splendid ornament, and threads the loveliest necklace and weaves the most exquisite stuff of mingled hues, and paces superbly in a garden of roses." But the same critic complains that the poet too often uses far-fetched metaphors and "Strings pearls and bricks together."[40] Two lines of his poetry are a good example of this ornate style.

> She shone forth like a moon and swayed like a moringa-bough,[41]
> And shed fragrance like ambergris, and gazed like a gazelle.[42]

Not all of the poetry of al-Mutanabbī was devoted to metaphors and word pictures, as some of his verses were of a serious nature, moralizing about human life.

The greatest philosopher among the poets was abū-al-'Alā' al-Ma'arrī,[43] the blind and heretical sage of Syria. One of his poems is of interest even for persons unfamiliar with Arabic, as some authorities think that it inspired Dante to write his *Divine Comedy*. This work entitled *Risālat al-Ghufrān* relates how

> Sheikh Aly Bin Mansour became ordained
> To take this gift divine and call it home.
> He chose some friends in heaven to entertain,
> To pass their time in most delightful mirth.
> He picked his friends to be from those well known
> For verse and prose, they had composed on earth.[44]

These lines explain how a man named Shaykh 'Alī was permitted to visit heaven, where he met famous men of times gone by. He conversed with some of the poets of the Pre-Islamic and early Islamic periods[45] seeing also al-Khalīl ibn-Aḥmad,[46] the

40. Nicholson *(Lit. Hist.)* p. 309, quoting al-Tha'ālibī.
41. Branch of the moringa tree.
42. Nicholson *(Lit. Hist.)* p. 310.
43. He lived from 973 to 1057, his home being Ma'arrat al-Nu'mān south of Aleppo. See Khallikān *(Biog. Dict.)* Vol. I, p. 94; Nicholson *(Lit. Hist.)* pp. 313-324.
44. Quoted from an unpublished translation of the *Epistle of Forgiveness*, which was written some time after 1033.
45. Zuhayr ibn-abī-Sulmā, 'Adī ibn-Zayd of al-Ḥīrah, Labīd ibn-Rabī'ah, al-A'shā abū-Basīr of the banū-Qays, Ḥassān ibn-Thābit, and other poets.
46. Already mentioned as the compiler of the first Arabic dictionary.

Prophet Muḥammad, the Prophet's uncle Ḥamzah and his famous daughter Fāṭimah. Then he went to the garden of evil spirits, where he had adventures with animals and ghosts. He also met numerous poets, eternally damned because they lived too early to enjoy the salvation of Islām, or held heretical ideas.[47] Finally, he returned to heaven, where, after meeting Adam and other celebrities, he enjoyed a beautiful damsel and the other joys of paradise.

The following verses from a poem of abū-al-'Alā' known as "al-Luzūmīyāt" can also be appreciated by persons unable to read Arabic, as the translation shows how modern in spirit the poet was, in spite of his blindness and medieval environment.

Now, mosques and churches—even a Kaaba Stone,
Korans and Bibles—even a martyr's bone,—
All these and many more my heart can tolerate,
For my religion's love and love alone.

To humankind, O Brother, consecrate
Thy heart, and shun the hundred sects that prate
About the things they little know about—
Let all receive thy pity, none thy hate.

'What is thy faith and creed,' they ask of me,
'And who art thou? Unseal thy pedigree.'—
I am the child of time, my tribe, mankind,
And now this world's my caravanseri.[48]

Although the Qur'ān is not classified as poetry or belles-lettres, it must not be forgotten that it has the same literary importance for the Muslims as Homer has for the Greeks. Unfortunately, it is impossible to translate the diction of the Qur'ān and the musical language of poetry, so as to do justice to the original Arabic, but for the Arabs themselves their literature is a rich treasury of beauty and inspiration.

In spite of the fact that the principal language of instruction during the Middle Ages was Arabic, it is well to bear in mind that some of the best medieval poetry was written as Persian rather than Arabic literature. Firdawsī, who died about 1025, wrote his great epic entitled the "Shāhnāmah," which inspired the Persians as the "Aeneid" did the Romans. The quatrains ascribed to the

47. Al-Khansā', Bashshār ibn-Burd, Imru'-al-Qays, 'Amr ibn-Kulthūm, 'Antar, and other poets.

48. Ma'arrī, al-, abū-al-'Alā', *(Luzūmīyāt)* trans. Amīn al-Riḥānī (Ṣādir Riḥānī, Beirut, 1944) pp. 72, 14, 79.

mathematician 'Umar Khayyām are well known by English speaking people as well as by Persians, because of FitzGerald's popular translation.

Shaykh Farīd-al-Dīn, nicknamed al-'Aṭṭār, is a good example of a mystic who wrote beautiful Persian poetry. He was a druggist, who died during the first part of the thirteenth century and, like many other religious thinkers, expressed his emotions in verse. An even more famous mystic was the great saint, Jalāl-al-Dīn al-Rūmī. Although he was born in Balkh in 1207, he was more intimately connected with Konia in Asia Minor,[49] where before he died in 1273 he founded the Mevlevi Order of Dervishes. During his years of travel and religious devotion, he composed some of the most beautiful poetry of the medieval period.

Sa'dī, who was born at Shīrāz about 1184, and also the great fourteenth century lyric poet Ḥāfiẓ, are so well known that it is only necessary to mention their names, in order to emphasize the importance of Persian poetry. Last but not least of these great classic poets of Persia was Jāmī,[50] who died during the year that Columbus discovered America.

The Crusades, which started thirty-eight years after the death of the poet abū-al-'Alā' al-Ma'arrī, were followed by devastating Mongolian invasions and four centuries of Ottoman rule. It is not surprising that, during these years of war and imperialism, Arabic culture lost so much of its vitality, that few literary masterpieces were produced.

We are now, however, living in the midst of an Arab awakening, when some poems, essays and stories of real value are being written. Because of this modern renaissance, literary courses are as much sought after in the schools of the twentieth century as they were in the medieval colleges and mosques.

Commentary

At the same time that the scholars were encouraging linguistic and literary studies, they developed Qur'ānic exegesis or commentary as the science of "al-tafsīr." As long as the Companions of the Prophet and their children were alive, they understood the background of the Qur'ān so well that they hesitated to corrupt the divine revelation by human interpretation. But after the

49. Iconium or Qunyā. The order is also known as that of al-Mawlawīyah or Whirling Dervishes.

50. Nūr-al-Dīn 'Abd-al-Raḥmān Jāmī, 1414-1492.

persons who had known the Prophet intimately had passed away, public opinion changed.

Because the authorized version of the Qur'ān lacked both historical sequence and explanatory notes, it was only possible to understand the revelations accurately by recalling what the Prophet himself and his closest associates had said about them. A century and a half after the Prophet's death, a great scholar like al-Aṣma'ī therefore felt free to study the traditions and to comment on the meaning of the Qur'ān as an act of piety. He was followed by other authorities, who developed commentary into a highly respected Muslim science.[51]

It was taken for granted that the explanation of the Qur'ān should be a matter of factual knowledge, rather than of personal opinion. Only a statement known to have been made by the Prophet himself, or by one of his wives or Companions was regarded as authoritative.[52] In order to prove that he was using a saying about the Qur'ān accurately, a commentator was accustomed to cite the names of all of the persons who had handed down the saying from the Prophet's own time.

The following quotation from the great commentary of al-Ṭabarī illustrates this procedure. The passage explains the meaning of the term "Yawm al-Dīn" contained in the opening passage of the Qur'ān.

> Mūsā ibn-Hārūn al-Hamdānī relates to us saying, 'Amr ibn-Ḥammād al-Qannād told us saying, Asbāṭ ibn-Naṣr al-Hamdānī passed on to us from Ismā'īl ibn-'Abd-al-Raḥmān al-Suddī from abū-Mālik from abū-Ṣāliḥ from ibn-'Abbās and from Murrah al-Hamdānī from ibn-Mas'ūd and people who were Companions of the Prophet . . . that Yawm al-Dīn is the Day of Judgment.[53]

The following is another example with the sources of the tradition omitted.

> While we were praying with the Prophet a caravan of camels arrived from Syria loaded with provisions. The Believers immediately rushed to the caravan, leaving only twelve men

51. See Nadīm, pp. 55, 33-35; Khaldūn (Quatremère) Part II, pp. 391-395; (Rosenthal) Vol. II, pp. 443-447.

52. This was *al-tafsīr bi'l-ma'thūr*. The Shi'ītes only accept traditions from members of the Prophet's family.

53. Translated from Ṭabarī, al-, *Tafsīr al-Qur'ān* (Dār al-Ma'ārif, 1958) Vol. I, p. 156. The Arabic original has after "Prophet" the words, "May Allah bless him and give him peace, for he is the king of Yawm al-Dīn, the Day of Reckoning."

with the Prophet. It was on this occasion that the verse was revealed, 'When they see some trading or distraction, they rush headlong to it and leave thee standing. Say, what is Allāh's is better than amusement and trading.'[54]

One reason why it is difficult to understand the Qur'ān is because certain passages abrogate the verses of preceding chapters. When for instance the Prophet first went to al-Madīnah, he taught his followers to face Jerusalem at times of prayer. The following traditions show how this injunction was modified.

> Aḥmad told us saying, abū-Aḥmad said, abū-al-Rabī' al-Sammān passed on to us from 'Āṣim ibn-'Ubayd-Allāh from 'Abd-Allāh ibn-'Āmir ibn-Rabī'ah from his father who said, 'We were with the Apostle of Allāh, may Allāh bless him and give him peace, one disagreeable night. When we camped the men taking stones made a place for worship where we could pray. When the morning broke, we realized that we had not prayed in the right direction, so we said 'Oh Apostle of Allāh last night when we prayed we faced the wrong direction!' Then Allāh exalted and glorious revealed 'The east and the west are Allāh's; whichever way you turn you face Allāh, for Allāh is omnipotent and all-knowing.'[55]

Another tradition explains that the direction of prayer[56] was further changed. The verse of the Qur'ān, "The east and the west are Allāh's; whichever way you turn you face Allāh," was later abrogated by the verse, "From whatever place you go forth, turn your face in the direction of the holy shrine."[57]

Some of the commentaries were written for students in a simple way, with the sources of the traditions omitted and the explanations given in brief form. The following remarks about Sūrah IV, verse 3 of the Qur'ān illustrate what one of these works was like.

Text	*Comment*
"If you fear that you cannot act fairly	that is deal justly

54. Translated from Bukhārī, al-, *El-Bokhārī, Les Traditions Islamiques* trans., O. Houdas and W. Marcais (Imprimerie Nationale, 1906) Vol. II, p. 7. The final verse is from the Qur'ān, Sūrah LXII, verse 11.

55. Ṭabarī *(Tafsīr)* Vol. II, p. 531. The quotation is from Sūrah II, verse 115, of the Qur'ān.

56. *Al-qiblah.*

57. Ṭabarī *(Tafsīr)* Vol. II, p. 529. The verse from Sūrah II, verse 149. The "holy shrine" refers to the Ka'bah at Makkah.

with the orphans	and that because of them some wrong will occur, and if they fear that you cannot treat them in a fair way along with other women if you marry them,
then wed	marry
what	whomever
is agreeable to you from among the women; double, triple or quadruple.	that is two at a time, three at a time or four at a time, but do not exceed that number.
But if you fear that you cannot be fair	to them in connection with expenses and allowances,
then just one	ought you to marry,
or	be content with
what your right hand possesses	of slaves not involving the obligations of wives."[58]

Here is a different type of comment from the same book, to explain the eleventh verse of Sūrah XXIV, which was revealed when the Prophet's wife 'Ā'ishah was accused of adultery.

Text	*Comment*
"Truly those who have come with a falsehood	fixed the lie abusing 'Ā'ishah, may Allāh be well pleased with her, the mother of the Believers.
are a group among you,	a group of the Believers said to be Ḥassān ibn-Thābit, 'Abd-Allāh ibn-Ubayy, Misṭaḥ and Ḥamnah bint-Jaḥsh.
Do not regard this	oh Believers not of the group,
as an evil for you, as it is a benefit for you."[59]	(A dozen lines follow to explain what happened to 'Ā'ishah.)

The comment explains that when 'Ā'ishah was returning with the Prophet from a raid, she dismounted at the rear of the

58. Jalālayn, (Jalāl-al-Dīn al-Maḥallī wa'Jalāl-al-Dīn al-Suyūṭī) *Tafsīr al-Qur'ān al-Aẓīm* (Dār Iḥyā' al-Kutub al-'Arabīyah, Cairo, 1920) Part I, p. 48.
59. *Ibid.*, Part II, p. 34.

caravan. Because her veil dropped off, she searched for it in the darkness. Failing to realize that she had not yet returned to the covered seat on her camel, her cameleer went on leaving her stranded. After waiting in vain for her associates to come back to look for her, she fell asleep. Then a man who happened to pass by took her to safety. The group took advantage of this incident to accuse her of immoral behavior.

Most of the commentaries are longer and more sophisticated than the book from which the last two examples have been taken. Abū-Ḥayyān, for instance, devotes eighteen pages to the short opening sūrah of the Qur'ān[60] and the following quotation from al-Bayḍāwī reveals a considerable breadth of scholarship.

Text	*Comment*
"O Maryam (Mary) truly Allāh gives you tidings of His Word, whose name is the Messiah, 'Īsā son of Maryam."[61]	"Messiah is his surname, being a title of honor like 'al-Ṣiddīq.' Its original form in Hebrew is Mashīḥā, meaning the 'Blessed'; 'Īsā being an abridged form of Īshū'. The derivation of the word is from 'masaḥa,' to rub, because he was anointed with a blessing, or with something that cleansed him from sin, or because he traversed the earth, not remaining in one place, or because Gabriel caressed him."[62]

A comment of a legal type from al-Nasafī is another example. It explains the procedure for remarriage as follows.

Text	*Comment*
"If he divorces her	a third time after two other times, and if she admits that

60. Ḥayyān, abū-, *Tafsīr al-Baḥr al-Muḥīṭ* (al-Sa'ādah Press, Cairo, 1910) pp. 14-32.

61. Sūrah III, verse 45 (40).

62. Bayḍāwī, al-, *Tafsīr al-Qāḍī al-Bayḍāwī* (Dār al-Sa'ādah 1896) Vol. I, p. 206; *Chrestomathia Baidawiana,* trans. D. S. Margoliouth (Luzac, 1894) p. 35.

	the annulment 'is a divorce for us'; (then follows a technical reference to the jurist al-Shāfi'ī.)
then she cannot legally become his again,	that is after the third pronouncement of divorce,
until she marries some husband other than him.	until she marries somebody different from him; the (second) marriage being confirmed both for the man and the woman. This shows that the (original) marriage has been ended, determining the formation of a new situation. (Here another technical note is inserted.)
Then if he divorces her	that is if the second husband divorces her, after a proper delay to see if she has a child,
there is no guilt attached to either of them,	either to the woman or her first husband;
if they reunite,	each one of them returning in marriage to the original mate,
provided they believe that they can abide by the ordiances of Allāh.	if it is their conviction that they will perform the duties of matrimony."
	(Then there is another reference of a technical nature.)[63]

The science of commentary became so important that people of different types were tempted to use it for their own selfish purposes. Thus the Fāṭimid Caliphs employed their system of allegorical interpretation[64] to prove that they alone had the divine right to rule the theocracy of Islām. In 929, moreover, there was a riot in Baghdād, because successors of the conservative jurist ibn-Ḥanbal disagreed with the free thinkers about the interpretation of the verse "Maybe your Lord will raise you to a position of

63. Nasafī, al-, *Tafsīr al-Nasafī* (al-Ḥusaynīyah Press, Cairo, 1925) Part I, p. 91, explaining Sūrah II, verse 230.

64. *Al-ta'wīl.*

great glory."[65] One party used exegesis to prove that the verse meant that Allāh would raise Muḥammad to sit on a throne by His side, while the other faction regarded this as blasphemy.

The mystics also used Qur'ānic verses to support their heterodox doctrines. Thus they confirmed their belief in ecstatic absorption by the Infinite when they quoted a beautiful passage ending with the words "Light, upon light; Allāh doth guide whom He wills to His light."[66]

During the twelfth century al-Zamakhsharī[67] developed his exegesis by linguistic studies rather than by too great a dependence upon tradition, using his great commentary to expound somewhat heretical ideas, whereas al-Bayḍāwī[68] a century later provided an orthodox counterpart.

Because groups like the Fāṭimids, Mu'tazilah, mystics and free thinkers used exegesis to uphold their heretical ideas, it became essential for Sunnite scholars to study commentary, so as to defend their orthodox tenets. The science of commentary or "al-tafsīr," therefore, became closely connected with dogmatic studies and was basic for an understanding of theology.

The principal uses of commentary, however, were to enable scholars to interpret the revelations for legal purposes, as well as to explain the Qur'ān for devotional reading. During the course of the centuries, thousands of commentaries were written and exegesis of the Qur'ān became one of the most important subjects of the curriculum.

Closely connected with this study was a technical science, which guided the mosque leaders and teachers in reading and reciting the Qur'ān in an accurate way. Especially during Ramaḍān, but also at other times, large groups of men and equally important groups of women have always frequented the mosques, to hear the Qur'ān read aloud. During the Middle Ages, when most of the people were illiterate, these readings were of great importance. The Qur'ān, moreover, has always been recited at family festivals and public celebrations, so that the art of rendering it correctly has great practical importance in Muslim communities. Accordingly, one of the subjects of the curriculum was "readings" or "al-qirā'āt."

65. Sūrah XVII, verse 79.

66. Sūrah XXIV, verse 35. See also Sūrah II, verse 156.

67. Abū-al-Qāsim Maḥmūd ibn-'Umar al-Zamakhsharī, 1075-1144, author of *al-Kashshāf 'an Ḥakā'iq al-Tanzīl.*

68. 'Abdallāh ibn-'Umar al-Bayḍāwī; died 1286 or soon afterwards; author of *Anwār al-Tanzīl wa-Asrār al-Ta'wīl.*

Readings

Even if a mosque leader or teacher was acquainted with the linguistic sciences and commentary, he was not always able to render the words of the Qur'ān accurately. Accordingly, it became necessary to develop this science of readings or "al-qirā'āt."

In Arabic there are small signs instead of vowels, while consonants like b, t, th, n, y, look alike, unless they have dots either over them or under them. In the same way r and z are identical, unless there is a dot over the z. As has already been mentioned, these marks to distinguish vowels and consonants were not used in early Islām. Thus it was possible to read Qur'ānic words in different ways.

Once, for instance, when he was talking with a colleague, the grammarian al-Māzinī said, "When I was a lad I recited to my father 'Thou seest the rain come forth from its clefts *(khilālihi).*' " Then the companion retorted, "If it were good form it would be 'Come forth from *khalalihi!*' " The authorized version of the Qur'ān has *khilālihi.*[69]

It is evident, therefore, that it was possible to read the sacred revelations of the Qur'ān in various ways, as the following examples more clearly explain.

A word in Sūrah VII, verse 48, might have been written *tastakbirūn* (you act haughtily) or *tastakthirūn* (you overdo it). Another word occurring in Sūrah IV, verse 94, could have been rendered *fa-tabayyanū* (investigate) or *fa-tathabbatū* (confirm), while a word in Sūrah XLVIII, verse 9, might equally well have been pronounced *tu'azzirūhu* (that you may penalize him), or *tu'azzizūhu* (that you may honor him).[70]

Because of such ambiguity there were almost as many ways of interpreting the divine revelation as there were men to recite it. This lack of uniformity became so serious during the reign of the Caliph al-Qāhir, that his two famous viziers[71] made it illegal to recite the Qur'ān according to systems other than those of seven

69. Nadīm, p. 45. Abū 'Uthmān al-Māzinī of al-Baṣrah, who died about 863 A.D. was talking with Abū Saddār al-Ghanawī. For the Qur'ānic rendering, see Sūrahs XXIV, verse 43, and XXX, verse 48.

70. Goldziher, Ignaz, *Madhāhib al-Tafsīr al-Islāmī,* trans. 'Abd-al-Ḥalīm al-Najjār (al-Khanjī Press, Cairo, 1955) pp. 9, 10, 11. See also Jeffery, Arthur, *Materials for the History of the Text of the Qur'ān* (Brill, Leiden, 1937) p. 232, 362.

71. Ibn-Muqlah and ibn 'Īsā, helped by the scholar ibn-Mujāhid, see Ḥittī *(Arabs)* p. 123; Jeffery, p. 1.

well known authorities.[72] All other methods of Qur'ānic reading were so strictly banned that one notorious heretic[73] was beaten and put in prison, because he insisted upon using a method of his own.

After consonant and vowel signs had been adopted and these seven methods of reading the Qur'ān had become formally recognized, the science of "al-qirā'āt," or readings, developed into a well defined study. It was supplemented by the art of "al-tajwīd," or intoning, which made it possible to chant the words of the Qur'ān so that the members of large congregations could hear and understand.

One of the excellent customs of Islām is the training of blind boys to intone the Qur'ān at festivals and services, so that they can become self-supporting.

This study of "readings" was an important subject of the curriculum in medieval times and is still taught to students expecting to be employed in mosques, as well as to blind boys, planning to be professional reciters of the Qur'ān.

Traditions

The scholars found out how to recite the Qur'ān accurately just as they learned to understand it, by studying the things which the Prophet said about the revelations and the way in which he applied them to everyday life. The subject dealing with these sayings and precedents of Muḥammad is called the "science of al-ḥadīth," or "traditions." As it forms a basis, not only for commentary and readings, but also for law and theology, it is one of the most important subjects of the curriculum.

The sayings of the Prophet must not be confused with the Qur'ān. The Prophet was occasionally subject to seizures, which turned him into a medium for the transmission of divine knowledge. The followers of Muḥammad believe that it was this revelation from Allāh which formed the Qur'ān. The words of the Qur'ān are not regarded by orthodox Muslims as coming from Muḥammad, but from God.

Except for his spells of prophetic seizure, Muḥammad was a normal person. The traditions recorded what he said and did during the majority of the time, when he spoke and acted as a normal human being, subject to the emotions of other men. As

72. Nadīm, pp. 28-31. Khaldūn (Quatremère) Part II, p. 388; (Rosenthal) Vol. II, p. 440; Bell, p. 49.
73. Nadīm, pp. 31, 32.

he himself explained, "When I tell you about your religion, receive it, but when I give you my personal opinion, then I am only a man."[74]

It is important, however, to realize that even when Muḥammad spoke as an ordinary individual, he was more capable than any one else to explain the meaning of the divine revelations. Accordingly, only a few years after the Prophet's death his son-in-law, 'Alī, and his cousin, ibn-al-'Abbās, started to collect the things which Muḥammad's relatives and associates remembered hearing him say, while he was still alive.

As one generation followed another, conscientious scholars feared that the sayings might become distorted. The persons quoting them did not always have good memories, sometimes being careless or even deliberately deceitful in repeating words attributed to the Prophet. The scholars, therefore, tried to sift out the authentic traditions, so as to codify them in written form. The process of seeking, analyzing, evaluating and recording quotations connected with the Prophet developed into this science called "al-ḥadīth."[75]

Some of the earliest traditions were included with biographical material about the Prophet and his Companions. Thus ibn-Isḥāq recorded many sayings and anecdotes in his life of Muḥammad, his example being followed by other historians when they wrote about the wars and heroes of Islām.[76]

The scholars divided a tradition into two parts: the "isnād" or chain of persons passing on a quotation, and the "matn" or content of what was originally said. The following example explains the nature of these two parts. First there is the "isnād,"—"Ibrāhīm ibn-al-Mundhir told us that Anas ibn-'Iyāḍ related to us saying that 'Ubayd-Allāh passed on to us from Khubayb ibn-'Abd-al-Raḥmān from Ḥafṣ ibn-'Āṣim from abū-Hurayrah, with whom may Allāh be well pleased, that the Apostle of Allāh, may Allāh bless him and give him peace, said"—then follows the "matn"—"Faith seeks al-Madīnah as a serpent seeks its hole."[77]

Another example quotes Aḥmad ibn-Ḥanbal as saying that "Abū-Mu'āwiyah passed on what Dāwūd ibn-abī-Hind related

74. Faḍl, M., *Sayings of the Prophet Muhammad* (Reform Society, Allahabad, 1924) Intr. p. xvii.

75. Khaldūn (Quatremère) Part II, pp. 395-406; (Rosenthal) Vol. II, pp. 447-463.

76. For ibn-Isḥāq see Guillaume *(Life of Muhammad).* Two early historians were ibn-Sa'd and al-Balādhurī.

77. Bukhārī, al-, *Ṣaḥīḥ al-Bukhārī,* edit., al-Kirmānī, (al-Miṣrīyah Press, 1934) Part IX, p. 67.

from abū-Ḥarb ibn-abī-al-Aswad from abū-Dharr, who stated that the Apostle of Allāh, may Allāh bless him and give him peace, said to us 'If one of you grows angry while standing, let him sit down, or perhaps his anger will cool off if he lies down.' "[78]

Politicians used the sayings of the Prophet to support their political claims, while judges used them to determine court decisions. It is no wonder therefore that pretenders to the throne, on the one hand, and dishonest lawyers on the other, were tempted to distort old traditions or to invent new ones. As the theologians also depended upon Muḥammad's sayings to confirm their doctrines and scholars tried to gain prestige by quoting as many traditions as possible, even the learned authorities were tempted to fabricate traditions for dishonest purposes. It is, moreover, likely that when Christians, Jews and Zoroastrians became converted to Islām, they confused popular texts and verses learned in childhood with the sayings repeated to them after they had become Muslims.

Because of this unsatisfactory state of affairs, conscientious scholars spent years in studying the reliability of the traditions, so as to compile collections of such quotations as their research led them to regard as genuine. Six of these collections are considered to be trustworthy, the most important one being that of al-Bukhārī, who travelled during sixteen years to places as far distant as Egypt and Afghānistān, interviewing scholars and sifting the traditions quoted to him. He prayed over each saying before he entered it in his book, seeking God's help to avoid mixing spurious with genuine quotations. As he was supposed to have selected only about 7,500 sayings from the half million quoted to him, it is appropriate for his collection to be called "al-Ṣaḥīḥ," or "The Sound." The work of Muslim ibn-al-Ḥajjāj was also considered reliable enough to be called by the same name.[79]

The experts evaluated traditions as "sound," "good" and "weak."[80] Scholars as painstaking as al-Bukhārī and Muslim

78. Dāwūd, abū-, *Sunan abī-Dāwūd* (al-Kastānīyah Press, Cairo, 1863) Part II, p. 186.

79. The compilers of the six collections and the years of their deaths are as follows:—

(1) Muḥammad ibn-Ismā'īl al-Bukhārī, 870 A.D.
(2) Muslim ibn-al-Ḥajjāj, 875 A.D.
(3) Abū-Dāwūd, 888 A.D.
(4) Al-Tirmidhī, 892 A.D.
(5) Ibn-Majah, 886 A.D.
(6) Al-Nasā'ī, 915 A.D.

80. *Ṣaḥīḥ, ḥasan, ḍa'īf.* For further information refer to Maḥmaṣānī, *Falsafāt al-Tashrī' fī al-Islām,* trans. Farḥāt J. Ziyādah (Brill, Leiden, 1961) p. 71.

used a very severe system to determine which sayings belonged to the first category of "sound" traditions. First of all they made certain that the quotation originated with a member of the Prophet's generation, known for honesty and good memory, and that it was endorsed by two other persons of integrity. Then they ascertained that a member of the second generation of Islām had passed on the tradition to Muslims of the third generation, with the confirmation of two other reliable persons. Finally, they required a "ḥāfiẓ," or authority skilled in remembering the traditions, and several other trustworthy men to transmit the saying to scholars of their own time.[81]

The best way to gain an appreciation of the importance of tradition is to study the table of contents of the *Ṣaḥīḥ* of al-Bukhārī, a translation of which is given in Appendix II at the back of the book.[82] The following quotations, moreover, serve as examples of the thousands of sayings, which form the basis of the science of al-ḥadīth.

To begin with there are some sayings about government. "The tyrant shall not enter into paradise." "When a governor regards his people with suspicion, he brings ruin to them." "The best of holy wars is when one speaks of justice in the presence of a despotic official."[83]

The next series of quotations illustrates how traditions affected legal procedure. "Abū-Lubābah proposed to give away all that he had to charity, but the Prophet said, 'A third will be enough in your case.' "[84] "Whoever is ignorant of medicine, but gives a drug, will be held responsible for what he does." "A vow which is sinful should not be fulfilled."[85]

With regard to military law, the "Apostle of Allāh forbade plundering and mutilation." "The Prophet forbade the killing of women and children."[86]

The following traditions determine who should own land, which has been neglected and reclaimed. "Whoever cultivates and inhabits a piece of land lacking an owner shall have the first claim

81. Naysābūrī, al-, *Al-Madkhal ilā Ma'rifat al-Iklīl,* edit., James Robson (Royal Asiatic Soc., Luzac, 1953), (Eng.) p. 14; (Arab.) p. 11.

82. For the Arabic titles, giving the contents of the six authoritative collections, see Wensinck, A. J., *A Handbook of Early Muhammadan Tradition* (E. J. Brill, 1927), pp. xi-xvi.

83. Faḍl, pp. 75, 76.

84. *Ibid.,* p. 127. This decision gave the legal heirs the right to two thirds of the estate.

85. *Ibid.,* pp. 117, 234.

86. Bukhārī *(Traditions)* Vol. II, p. 151.

to it." "Dead land belongs to whoever brings it to life. There is no right to take it (away from him)." "Whoever cultivates and lives on land, deserted and neglected by the owner, shall possess it."[87]

Several examples illustrate what financial instructions about usury and speculation were like. "Do not exchange gold for gold except for equal value, or silver for silver except for equal value, but exchange gold for silver and silver for gold as you wish." "The Apostle of Allāh forbade selling dates before they were ripe and when asked what ripe meant he said, 'When they are red or yellow, that is edible.' "[88] Another tradition quotes abū-Sa'īd as telling that the Prophet forbade the sale of cloth without an opportunity to examine it.[89]

The fourth subject dealt with by al-Bukhārī in his great collection was ritualitsic purity. He handed down a tradition that ibn-'Abbās saw the Prophet perform his ablutions before prayer in the following way.

> He washed his face, taking a handful of water and rinsing with it while inhaling. Then he did the same thing with a handful in his other hand, again washing his face with it. After that he took up a handful of water and, after washing his right hand, he bathed his left hand, using a second handful of water. Then after wiping his head he took a handful of water to sprinkle his right foot, washing it. Next he took another handful of water and washed his foot, that is his left foot.[90]

A second tradition concerned with ritualistic purity, and referring to the ordinance to bathe after sexual intercourse, was quoted from 'Ā'ishah when she said, "I used to wash with the Prophet, may Allāh bless him and give him peace, using only one vessel, a piece of pottery called a farq."[91] 'Ā'ishah also said that the Prophet ordered the taking of a bath not only after sexual intercourse, but also on Fridays, in case of cupping and after washing a corpse.[92]

Traditions about marriage, divorce and inheritance are of a supplementary nature, as the Qur'ān itself gives such detailed

87. Faḍl, p. 105, with wording modified.
88. Bukhārī *(Traditions)* Vol. II, pp. 39, 43.
89. 'Alī, Muḥammad, *A Manual of Ḥadīth* (Maktaba Ahmadiya, Lahore) p. 296.
90. Bukhārī, al-, *Kitāb al-Jāmi' al-Ṣaḥīḥ*, edit. M. L. Krehl (E. J. Brill, 1860), Vol. I, p. 49.
91. Bukhārī, al-, *(Traditions)* Vol. I, p. 112.
92. 'Alī *(Manual of Ḥadīth)* p. 60, paraphrased.

instructions about these matters. A few quotations, however, must be included to show what the Prophet's sayings about women were like. "A man proposed marriage to a woman of the Anṣār. The Prophet said to him, 'Have you seen her?' The man replied, 'No.' Then 'Go,' said the Prophet, 'and see her.' "

"A widow shall not be married until she is consulted, nor a virgin until after her approval is asked for. They said, 'And how shall she give her permission?' The Prophet replied, 'She will keep silent.' "

"The adulterer who has been beaten shall only marry his counterpart," that is an adulteress punished in a similar way. "When selling a slave 'Alī separated a mother from her child, but the Prophet forbade this, cancelling the sale." "When the slave girl of a man gives birth to a child by that man, she becomes free after his death."[93]

According to Islām one of the great sins is the misuse of trust funds, especially those belonging to orphans. Several sayings show how the Prophet felt about this matter. "When trusts are wasted, then wait for the Judgment." "Restore the trusts of those who put faith in you and do not deal falsely with him who deals falsely with you."[94]

A few illustrations suggest how traditions can form the basis of theological dogmatism. "No servant (of God) who says 'There is no deity but Allāh' and then dies, will fail to enter heaven." "The Prophet said, 'The man who will have the best chance to gain my intercession on the Day of Resurrection will be he who says 'There is no deity but Allāh,' with purity in his heart." This saying is important both because of its mention of intercession and its promise of salvation. In connection with his own prophethood Muḥammad said, "Do not praise me as the Christians extol the Son of Mary, for truly I am but God's servant. Call me therefore the servant of Allāh, and His apostle."

Islām is said to be fatalistic, but once "A man asked the Prophet, 'In trusting Allāh should I tie my camel by the legs, or should I let him go free, relying upon Allāh?' The Prophet replied, 'First tie its legs and then trust Allāh.' "[95]

Throughout the history of Islām great spiritual leaders like al-Ghazzālī and Shaykh Muḥammad 'Abduh[96] have led reform

93. Faḍl, pp. 114, 113, 115, 211.
94. *Ibid.*, p. 221.
95. *Ibid.*, pp. 50, 66, 88.
96 Al-Ghazzālī was the great mystic, saint and scholar of Persia and 'Irāq, who lived 1058—1111. Muḥammad 'Abduh was the leading scholar of Egypt. He was born in 1849 and died in 1905.

movements. Muslims believe that their work was foretold by the Prophet when he said, "Truly Allāh will raise up for this people, at the beginning of every hundred years, one who will revive their religion for them."[97]

At the same time the Prophet urged his followers not to permit saint worship. This warning is taken seriously by the Wahhābī, who forbid worship at saints' tombs. What Muḥammad said was, "Oh Allāh, make not my grave an idol to be worshipped. Severe is the wrath of Allāh against people who make the graves of their prophets places of worship."[98]

'Ubaydah related that the Prophet said that whatever a man's actions might have been previously, Allāh will accept him into paradise, provided he "Testifies that there is no divinity except Allāh, unique without associates; that Muḥammad is His devotee and His messenger; that Jesus is also the devotee of Allāh, as well as His messenger and His word formed in the womb of Mary as a divine emanation; that heaven is true and that hell is also true."[99] "The grievous sins are polytheism, disobedience to parents, the killing of those who breathe and swearing falsely."[100]

Many of the traditions describe the way in which the Prophet acted, setting an example for his associates. He was once seen "Wiping the face of his horse with his robe. When he was questioned about this he said, 'During the night I had a reprimand from Allāh concerning my horse!' " With the same fondness for animals he did not allow cutting a horse's forelock, mane or tail.[101] On another occasion a bier passed by the Prophet and he stood up. It was said to him, "Verily, it is the bier of a Jew." The Prophet remarked, "Was he not a human being?"

"The Prophet cursed the giver of bribes and the receiver of bribes in deciding legal cases."[102]

One tradition tells how he used to love and kiss little children. Other sayings explain his dislike of the nudity of pagan times. 'Ā'ishah, for instance, told the following anecdote about her sister. "Asmā', a daughter of abū-Bakr, came to see the Prophet with just a thin cloth over her. The Prophet turned aside from her saying, 'O Asmā'! when a woman reaches your age it is not right for any part of her to be visible except this and this' (pointing to her face and hands)." In this same connection the Prophet said, "Let no

97. Faḍl, p. 187.
98. *Ibid.*, p. 73.
99. Bukhārī *(Traditions)* Vol. II, p. 516.
100. Faḍl, p. 206.
101. *Ibid.*, p. 15.
102. *Ibid.*, p. 24.

man look upon the secret parts of another man, nor a woman on the secret parts of another woman."[103]

There are many traditions explaining how prayer should be conducted. Most of them are too long and technical to be quoted, but the following sayings are included, as they throw light on the Prophet's point of view. Anas said that 'Ā'ishah had some "Cloth with patterns on it, which she was storing in a corner of her room. One day the Prophet said, 'Take this material away, as the designs distract me when I come to pray.' " Maymūnah related that "The Apostle of Allāh used to pray on a little mat." "According to abū-Hurayrah the Prophet said, 'When Ramaḍān comes the doors of heaven open.' " The Prophet, moreover, told the women not to pray during menstruation.[104]

On another occasion Muḥammad said, "All the earth is a place for worship, except cemeteries and baths." He loved to pray in the garden and also told people to say their prayers in their houses, as well as at the mosque. Some of the traditions record the words of the Prophet's prayers, so that his followers can memorize them for their own use. The sayings also tell how Muḥammad stood, bowed and prostrated himself in prayer. It is evident, however, that he did not demand a rigid ritual for worship. One man said, "I have seen the Prophet when he was praying lying down," and another person told how Muḥammad prayed with his granddaughter on his lap.[105]

Several quotations tell how the Prophet used to salute women and children in a kindly way as he passed by them, although this was not the custom in Arabia. There is also the record that the "Prophet of Allāh used to take his womenfolk with him on raids. They nursed the wounded and were given portions of the spoils."[106]

Although the traditions are as a rule studied in connection with commentary, theology and law, many of them are especially valuable because of their spiritual and ethical significance. Sayings of this sort deal with humility, simplicity, forgiveness, generosity, kindness to parents, servants and slaves, industriousness and service for others. They condemn sins like adultery, sodomy, usury, drunkenness and suicide. They encourage normal living instead of asceticism and moderation rather than excess, prescribing mar-

103. *Ibid.*, p. 129.
104. Bukhārī *(Traditions)* Vol. I, pp. 143, 146, 608, 122.
105. Faḍl, pp. 166, 175, 176.
106. *Ibid.*, pp. 197, 238.

riage with fair treatment and kindness in the home. They exhort men to avoid divorce and to handle their family finances honestly. They emphasize the importance of faith, consecration and worship, which must be sincere rather than for outward show, making it evident that true religion is not a matter of law and ritual, but of humble trust in God and obedience to His ordinances. The following examples of these ethical traditions are so popular that it is worth while to quote them, even if their origins may not always be entirely clear.

"Do you love your Creator? Love your fellowmen first." "Man is the brother of man, whether he likes him or not." "All creatures are the family of God, the most beloved by Him being the most useful to His family."[107]

One sixteenth century author quoted a number of sayings about good disposition, reflecting a right attitude towards life. "The believers who are the most perfect in faith are those who are the happiest in disposition." "A good disposition is a bond of friendship from the mercy of Allāh." "A good disposition melts offenses as the sun melts ice." "He who has a good disposition will receive the same reward as one who has merit from fasting and prayer." "The best of the good is an excellent disposition."[108]

The Prophet praised wisdom when he said, "Pursue knowledge, (religious) even though it be to China." "The ink of the learned is as precious as the blood of the martyrs." "Honoring a learned man is worth honoring seventy prophets." "It is better to teach one hour in the night than to pray the whole night through."[109]

'Uthmān ibn-Maẓ'ūn vowed that "He would stand up in prayer all night, fast all day long forever and never marry a woman." The Prophet, however, asked him to follow his own example, saying "I both sleep and pray. Although I fast, I eat. I also marry." "Truly you have a duty to society and a duty to your neighbor and a duty to yourself. So fast but eat, and pray but sleep."[110]

Some of the sayings attributed to the Prophet are so much like the words of the Gospels, that critical scholars have tried to find a connection between them. The following traditions illustrate the nature of this problem. "Feed the hungry, visit the sick and free

107. *Ibid.*, p. 67. Compare pp. 148, 149.

108. Donaldson, D. M., *Studies in Muslim Ethics* (SPCK, London, 1953), p. 79. The sayings are quoted from ibn-Mutaqqī, who died in 1567. Good disposition is *ḥusn al-khulq*.

109. Sayings attributed to the Prophet, often quoted by Muslim educators.

110. Faḍl, p. 3.

the captive." "He who humbles himself before Allāh will Allāh exalt." "He who is proud and haughty will Allāh render contemptible." "He who prays to make a show, associates (himself as another deity) with Allāh. He who gives alms to make a show, associates (himself) with Allāh." "I never knew the Prophet to be asked about any case of retaliation, without his commanding forgiveness." "Whoever comes to my place of prayer, let him come for good works; either to learn or to teach them."[111]

These examples can only give a very superficial idea of the extent and importance of the "science of al-ḥadīth," or traditions. The subject is such a vast one that a course dealing with al-Bukhārī required two hundred and ten lessons during two years of study.[112] It was, however, necessary for a student to master the subject, in order to understand commentary, law and theology.

The Law

During the first century of Islām the Muslims found that they must administer an empire stretching from the Atlantic to the Himalayas. One of their most important problems was to form a judicial system, which was based upon the Qur'ān but at the same time suited to the needs of vast numbers of converts and subject peoples. The development of this system produced the "science of al-fiqh" or law, the mastery of which was the goal of many a student.[113]

When speaking about Muslim law, Shaykh al-Sha'rānī explained that the

> Qur'ān is the constitution, or religious and civil charter of the Muslim populations, according to which there is no place for establishing new laws of a general nature. All that remains is to develop and elaborate the existing legislation, seeking whatever contains the germs of evolution and giving precision and sanction to the ordinances, in accordance with the spirit and principles attributed to the Prophet.[114]

111. *Ibid.*, pp. 68, 80, 200, 191, 167.

112. Tritton *(Musl. Educ.)* p. 156.

113. The Muslim legal system is *al-Sharī'ah*. It includes the study called *al-fiqh,* which is often translated as jurisprudence, but is more properly rendered as the law, and also *uṣūl al-fiqh,* which deals with the sources and means of arrival at the law.

114. Sha'rānī, al-, *Balance de la Loi Musulmane,* trans., Perron (Imprimerie Orientale, Alger, 1898), p. 22. See also Intr. p. xviii.

In other words Muslim law did not spring from the source of human experience, but according to the Islamic doctrine was received by revelation from Allāh. Its principal foundation stones are the ordinances occurring in the Qur'ān, a few examples of which are given in the following paragraphs.[115]

> Never should a believer kill a believer, and if it happens by mistake, compensation is due. If one so kills a believer, it is ordained that he should free a believing slave and pay compensation to the deceased's family, unless they remit it freely. If the deceased belonged to a people at war with you and he was a believer, the freeing of a slave is enough. If he belonged to a people with whom you have a treaty of mutual alliance, compensation should be paid to his family and a believing slave set free. For those who find this beyond their means there is prescribed a fast for two months in succession, by way of repentence to Allāh. (Sūrah IV, verse 92.)

The ordinances about food are too long to quote in detail, but in general it is stated that no meat is forbidden "Unless it be dead, or blood poured forth, or the flesh of swine." (Sūrah VI, verse 145.)

In other passages it is also made clear that a Muslim must not eat the flesh of an animal sacrificed to a false god, killed by a blow or fall, gored to death, or slain by beasts of prey.[116]

Some of the familiar passages of the Qur'ān contain instructions for the daily life of the community.

> As for a thief, male or female, cut off his or her hand. But if the thief repents after his crime and amends his conduct, Allāh turneth to him with forgiveness. (Sūrah V, verses 41 and 42.)

> Allāh will not call you to account for what is futile in your oaths, but He will call you to account for your deliberate oaths. For expiation feed ten needy persons, according to the average scale of food for your families, or reclothe them, or give a slave his freedom. If that is beyond your means, then fast for three days. (Sūrah V, verse 92.)

> They ask you concerning wine and gambling. Say: in them is great sin. (Sūrah II, verse 219.)

115. The translation is based on the A. Yūsuf 'Alī edition of the Qur'ān, Hafner Publishing Co., 1946, with certain modifications.

116. Compare Merchant, Muḥammad V., *A Book of Quranic Laws* (Ashraf, Lahore, 1947), pp. 111, 120.

> Allāh has permitted trade and forbidden usury. (Sūrah II, verse 275.)
>
> To orphans restore their property. Do not substitute worthless things for their good ones or devour their substance by mixing it with your own. (Sūrah IV, verse 2.)
>
> Give full measure when you measure, and weigh with an honest balance. (Sūrah XVII, verse 35.)
>
> Allāh thus directs you regarding your children: for a male a portion equal to that of two females. If there are only daughters, two or more, their share is two thirds of the inheritance; if only one her share is half. (Sūrah IV, verse 11.)

This verse is followed by detailed instructions for the shares of the inheritance assigned to parents, wives, brothers and sisters, when the children are deceased and also in other cases.

> Do not marry women whom your fathers have married . . . Prohibited to you are your mothers, daughters, sisters, aunts, nieces, foster-mothers who gave you suck, foster-sisters, mothers-in-law, step daughters under your guardianship, born of your wives with whom you have had sex relations; there being no prohibition if there have not been sex relations; the wives of your own sons, or two sisters at the same time. (Sūrah IV, verses 22 and 23.)

The laws for divorce are given in great detail. A pregnant woman who is divorced must await the birth of her child, so as to be sure to which husband the baby belongs, before she is allowed to marry again. Even a woman who is not pregnant must wait for a period of three months before remarriage. Rules for this procedure and similar matters are explained in a technical way. (Sūrah II, verses 226 to 242.)

In the scorching heat of Arabia the people wore so few garments that the Qur'ān gave instructions for modest behavior.

> Say to the believing women that they should lower their gaze and guard their private parts; that they should not display any of their ornaments except the apparent ones; that they should draw their coverings over their bosoms, not displaying their ornaments except to their husbands, fathers, fathers-in-law, sons and step sons, brothers and brothers' sons, sisters' sons, women, female slaves, men servants devoid of sexual desire, and children unconscious of sex. (Sūrah XXIV, verse 31.)

> The woman and the man guilty of adultery, flog each one of them with a hundred stripes . . . Those who launch a charge against chaste women, not producing four witnesses to support their accusations, flog them with eighty stripes. (Sūrah XXIV, verses 2 and 4.)

Qur'ānic passages such as these form the first source of legal knowledge. The second source is the "sunnah," composed of the sayings and precedents of the Prophet Muḥammad, who at al-Madīnah was a judge as well as a religious leader. In settling disputes between his tribesmen he relied to a great extent upon their local customs. The revelations of the Qur'ān did not do away with the old laws, but supplemented and modified them by means of new principles for progress and spiritual living. Thus the sayings and precedents of the Prophet show how he applied the revealed ordinances of the Qur'ān to the problems of everyday life.

Muḥammad's successors were obliged to deal not only with the Muslims themselves, but also with the people whom they conquered. Although a Muslim general, with a judge[117] to help him, was chiefly responsible for administering the ordinances of the Qur'ān among his own Muslims, he was also obliged to settle legal disputes between his Muslims and members of the subject races.[118] The Muslim authorities, therefore, must have studied the ancient legal codes, deriving practices from them. Thus, for instance, the Muslims had a clerk of the court, similar to a type of Persian Sāsānian official, and a "muḥtasib" like the Byzantine "agoranomos." Although Beirut was a great center of Roman law, supplying two jurists named Dorotheus and Anatolous to help draw up the Justinian Code, the Muslim authorities at Damascus were not as much influenced as one would expect by the Roman jurists in near-by cities like Beirut and Antioch.[119]

During the Umayyad period, when the capital was at Damascus, the judge was unable to render decisions in an independent way. Because he served as legal advisor and secretary to the governor, the judiciary was not separated from the political

117. *Al-qāḍī.*

118. The subject races were allowed to settle their private affairs among themselves by their old Roman, Coptic, Sāsānian, Talmudic and Melkite codes.

119. Consult Khaddūrī and Liebesny, *Law in the Middle East* (Middle East Inst., 1955). pp. 35-42 and 337; Macdonald, D. B. *Development of Muslim Theology, Jurisprudence and Constitutional Theory,* (Routledge, 1903) pp. 84, 85; Maḥmaṣānī, pp. 136-145.

administration. During the last part of the eighth century, however, when the 'Abbāsids were ruling at Baghdād, the judiciary became more perfectly organized. At least in theory the judge gave his decisions independently of politics, so that the legal authorities were able to develop the law as a systematic science.

The Prophet was reported to have said, "There are three classes of judges: one man recognizes the right and decides accordingly, this man goes to paradise; another one recognizes the right but goes in for wrong in his decision, this man goes to hell; and the third decides the cases of men in ignorance, he also goes to hell."[120]

As some of the judges lacked the technical knowledge required to form court decisions, the custom developed of appointing an expert to serve as a consultant. This consultant came to be called "al-muftī," his expert advice being "al-fatwā." Ibn-Khallikān gives a good example of what a fatwā was like. Abū-al-Ṭāhir al-Silafī asked for the expert opinion of abū-al-Ḥasan al-Ḥarrāsī concerning a point discussed at the Niẓāmīyah College. "What does the imām (whom God may favour!) say to this: a man willed one third of his property to the learned and to the jurisconsults; are the writers of the traditions included in the legacy or not? Under this question the shaikh wrote as follows. 'They are and why should they not?' has not the Prophet said,—'He who, for the advantage of my people, preserves forty traditions relating to their religion, shall be raised up by God, on the day of resurrection, as a jurisconsult and a learned man.' "[121]

During the early years of Islām, when the traditions were still unclassified and the law was in a primitive state, it was not easy for a judge to give a decision. The things which Muḥammad said and did were reported in such a variety of ways that there was much ambiguity. Jābir, for instance, said that when the Prophet was on one of his military raids he let the Muslims use the utensils of the infidels for eating and drinking. 'Ā'ishah, on the other hand, reported that the Prophet forbade them to use these utensils, while abū-Tha'labah recorded that the Prophet told the Muslims not to use Christian utensils, except at times of real necessity, when it was permissible to wash and use them.[122]

During the first Islamic generation, therefore, the judges were obliged to form their decisions by means of individual deduction and personal opinion,[123] as it was impossible to find instructions

120. Quoted from Faḍl, p. 90.

121. Khallikān *(Biog. Dict.)* Vol. II, p. 229. The incident occurred at the beginning of the 12th Cent.

122. Sha'rānī, pp. 19, 20.

in the Qur'ān and the sunnah to fit every case that appeared in court.

A paper written by a Syrian jurist explains that

> The learned al-Shahrastānī in his book "Al-Milal wa'l-Niḥal" says, 'In matters related to worship and behavior, events and incidents are uncountable and inexhaustible. For we know that no specific provision exists for every individual event, and that this would be inconceivable. So since provisions are finite and events are infinite, and since what is finite cannot include what is infinite, it is clear that *al-ijtihād,* or deduction and analogy, should be authoritative, so that there can be a juristic opinion to govern each individual case.'[124]

This word "al-ijtihād" represents an important principle of Muslim law. The best way to explain what it means is to quote a conversation, which Muslim scholars record as having taken place when the Prophet sent Mu'ādh ibn-Jabal to al-Yaman as a teacher and judge.

> The Prophet asked, 'What are your references for framing judgments, O Mu'ādh?' He replied, 'The Book of Allāh.' 'But,' the Prophet said, 'If it makes no provision for the case?' 'Then' said Mu'ādh, 'I will refer to the sunnah of His Apostle.' 'But if there too,' the Prophet continued, 'no provision exists?' 'I would apply my own studied opinion' said Mu'ādh, 'rather than to let the case go by default.' The Prophet approved this answer of Mu'ādh, saying 'Praise be to Allāh, who has inspired the envoy of His Apostle so that he can act in accordance with His satisfaction.'[125]

A good example has come down to us showing how a legal practice could be developed by this sort of personal common sense, which was the basis of individual opinion and analogy. This illustration has to do with the question of protecting the legal heirs by limiting the size of a bequest unfavorable to their interests. As the matter was not definitely determined by the Qur'ān, it had to be settled without the help of revelation. A man on his death bed tried to free his six slaves, but in accordance with a saying of the Prophet the local governor drew lots, so as to permit only two of the slaves to be set free. The other four slaves were retained to form part of the two thirds portion of the

123. *Al-ijtihād wa'l-ra'y.*

124. Zarqā, al-, Muṣṭafā, paper presented at the Int. Islamic Colloquium, Lahore, 1958, pp. 3, 4.

125. *Ibid.,* p. 2.

estate due to be distributed to the legal heirs. Thus the precedent was confirmed to limit the size of a bequest to one third of the estate.[126]

Due to their constant wars with the Emperor at Constantinople, the Umayyad Caliphs were greatly concerned with fiscal and military affairs. Land reclamation, the currency, control of the bazaars and other matters of public concern were, therefore, included in their legal system along with questions of taxation and inheritance. The Prophet's rules for division of the spoils of war had to be adapted to large scale campaigns. At the same time the penal ordinances for acts condemned by the Qur'ān and indemnities for injuries required adjustment.

When, moreover, many pagans, Christians, Jews and Zoroastrians were converted to Islām, exchanging their communal codes for Muslim law, it was inevitable that ancient customs[127] should enter into the everyday life of Islām. Although these usages did not form part of the Qur'ānic law, the Muslim jurists allowed many of them to influence their legal system.

In order to determine what was legal and what was illegal, the experts divided actions into five categories: (a) required, (b) designated, but not to be punished if neglected, (c) permitted, (d) disapproved, but not to be punished, (e) to be punished.[128]

As the associates of the Prophet settled in widely separated localities, their descendants formed numerous schools of thought in different parts of the Muslim world. Al-Madīnah was one of the first centers of legal study, being connected with the names of a number of well known authorities. Another center was al-Kūfah in 'Irāq, while Syria and Lebanon also made contributions under the leadership of scholars like al-Awzā'ī.[129] The Shī'ites and members of various sects inevitably had their own judicial interpretations, differing from those of the Sunnites.

The legal system developed by these early jurists is called "al-Sharī'ah," which in former times was comprehensive enough to serve the community in connection with all of its activities. A

126. See Schacht, Joseph, *The Origins of Muhammadan Jurisprudence* (Clarendon Press, 1950) p. 201. The governor was Abān ibn-'Uthmān of al-Madīnah. Refer to tradition quoted in section on al-ḥadīth, "A third will be enough in your case."

127. *Al-'ādah wa'l-'urf.*

128. The Arabic terms are (a) farḍ or wājib, (b) mandūb or mustaḥabb, (c) jā'iz or mubāḥ, (d) makrūh, (e) ḥarām. See Macdonald *(Dev. Muslim)* pp. 70-73.

129. Abū-'Umār 'Abd-al-Raḥmān al-Awzā'ī, 707-774 A.D., See Nadīm, p. 227. For brief accounts of the development of the law, see Maḥmaṣānī, p. 15 ff., and Mez, p, 211 ff.

despotic ruler is constantly tempted to issue an administrative edict,[130] so as to increase his own power at the expense of his subjects. Throughout Muslim history the Sharī'ah has served as a divinely given constitution, discouraging tyrants from treating their people in an illegal way. As has already been mentioned, the study of judicial matters connected with al-Sharī'ah developed the "science of al-fiqh" or the law. This field of professional study has been defined as the knowledge of the rights and obligations derived from the Qur'ān and traditions, or agreed upon by the scholars; the "Science of all things human and divine," prescribing "Everything that a man shall do to God, to his neighbor and to himself."[131] Although there is no true codification of Muslim law in our modern sense, the academic treatises written about judicial matters serve as codes for practical purposes.

Hundreds of scholars took part in the development of Muslim law, but only four of their codes have been formally adopted by Sunnite Islām.[132] The Muslims using these codes form the four official schools of orthodox law. There is also the Shī'ite law employed in Irān and other Shī'ite regions.

The different sects of Shī'ites, like the people of Persia, the Zaydīyah in al-Yaman and the Ismā'īlīyah, have legal codes of their own. In general they differ from the orthodox Sunnite codes, because they claim that only lineal descendants of the Prophet have the right to rule the world of Islām. They also have less important variations in connection with marriage, the observation of feasts and other matters. The great majority of Muslims, however, are governed by the Sunnite systems. The following paragraphs explain briefly what the four Sunnite codes of law represent and how they originated.

1. The Ḥanafī code was instituted by abū-Ḥanīfah,[133] who lived during a stormy period of history, when the 'Abbāsid revolution brought a new dynasty into power. He was a man of tawny complexion, fairly tall, handsome, eloquent and scholarly. After starting life as a silk merchant of al-Kūfah he went to Baghdād,

130. The edict, or *al-qānūn,* was not based on the Qur'ān or traditions and was apt to be used in a despotic way.

131. Fyzee, A. A. A., *Outlines of Muhammadan Law* (Oxford Univ. Press, 1955) p. 17; Macdonald *(Dev. Muslim)* p. 66. See also Khaldūn, (Quatremère) Part III, p. 1, ff. (Rosenthal) Vol. III, pp. 3-30.

132. The Sunnites have been loyal to the official caliphs, whereas the Shī'ites claim that the caliph must be a lineal descendant of the Prophet.

133. Abū-Ḥanīfah al-Nu'mān ibn-Thābit; see Khallikān *(Biog. Dict.)* Vol. III, pp. 555-565; Nadīm, pp. 201, 202; Khaldūn (Quatremère) Part III, p. 7; (Rosenthal) Vol. III, p. 6.

where he became a great legal authority about whose persecutions and virtues numerous legends were formed. He was more of a scholar than a practical judge, his influence being chiefly due to his lecturing, as his students spread his ideas far and wide. His system did not result from the demands of court trials, but was a theoretical attempt to meet all contingencies. He died seventeen years after the founding of the 'Abbāsid régime, being buried at Baghdād in 767 when he was seventy years old.

Abū-Ḥanīfah did not depend entirely upon the Qur'ān and the traditions. He gave up the usages of nomadic Arabia, substituting ordinances suited to settled life. He interpreted the Qur'ān largely by means of analogy and similar methods,[134] as the following example illustrates. Sūrah XXIV, verse 4 of the Qur'ān gives the judgment that those who launch a charge against a woman and do not produce four people to witness her adultery should be flogged with eighty stripes. By means of a tradition about 'Alī and by analogy, abū-Ḥanīfah determined that a fourfold confession could take the place of four witnesses.

The disciples of abū-Ḥanīfah compiled numerous books, developing his system to meet the demands of the vast realm of Islām. His code is still popular in Central Asia, the northern part of the Indian Peninsula, as well as among certain communities in Egypt and other places. Formerly it was the principal code of the Ottoman Empire.

2. The Mālikī code originated with Mālik ibn-Anas,[135] who lived at al-Madīnah from about 715 to 795 and was a tall, blond man, with a large bald head and closely clipped moustache. He was so pious that he refused to ride a horse in the city where the Prophet was buried. He gained great popularity when, due to a political dispute, the governor had him lashed and his arm stretched until his shoulder was dislocated.

In addition to the Qur'ān and traditions, Mālik permitted certain local practices of al-Madīnah,[136] as well as his own form of individual reasoning and a principle called "al-ijmā'," or consensus of opinion. He interpreted this principle as referring to agreement between the authorities of the early period of Islām,

134. He used *al-ra'y,* or individual reasoning, and *al-qiyās,* or analogy. He also employed *al-istiḥsān,* a method to settle legal cases according to what is preferable for the community. See Schacht, pp. 98-137.

135. He was abū-'Abdallāh Mālik ibn-Anas; see Nādīm, pp. 198, 199; Khallikān *(Biog. Dict.)* Vol. II, p. 545.

136. The local practice was *al-'amal,* the form of reasoning *al-istiṣlaḥ,* or community improvement.

rather than to a consensus of opinion of the jurists of later times. He is famous for his great collection of traditions, agreements about judicial opinions and legal reasoning.[137] His code, which is more practical and less theoretical than that of abū-Ḥanīfah, is still used in Upper Egypt and parts of North Africa.

3. The Shāfi'ī code was inspired by the life and work of a great jurist named al-Shāfi'ī.[138] Although he studied with Mālik at al-Madīnah, he spent most of his life at Baghdād at the time of Hārūn al-Rashīd. In 815 he went to Egypt where five years later he died. His domed tomb, still standing, is one of the important monuments of modern Cairo.

A valuable contribution of al-Shāfi'ī was the determining of the "uṣūl al-fiqh," or four legitimate sources for the development of the law, referred to in English as the fundamentals, roots or principles of the law.[139] The study called "uṣūl al-fiqh" is an essential subject of the curriculum, taught in the form of jurisprudence. The four sources dealt with by this subject are as follows:

(a) The Qur'ān, which is the most important basis of justice, as it is the revealed word of Allāh, the divine legislation serving as the true source of the law.

(b) Second in importance to the Qur'ān is the "sunnah," that is the sayings and precedents of the Prophet, explaining how Muḥammad interpreted and applied the Qur'ānic ordinances. Even if a saying of the Prophet did not interpret the revelation as one might expect, it was to be followed as Muḥammad knew better than anyone else what the Qur'ānic verses really meant. In fact al-Shāfi'ī held that a tradition could not be officially accepted for legal purposes, unless it told what Muḥammad himself said or did. He differed from some of the earlier jurists, because he believed that the sayings and actions of the Companions of the Prophet were not necessarily authoritative.

(c) Consensus of opinion, or "al-ijmā'," was the third source of the law honored by al-Shāfi'ī. For him it was not limited to the agreements of the Prophet's time, but included concurrence of the scholars of his own day, most of whom were in 'Irāq.

137. *Al-Muwaṭṭā'*.

138. Abū- 'Abdallāh Muhammad ibn-Idrīs al-Shāfi'ī, born at Ghazzah, 767, died at Cairo 820. See Khallikān *(Biog. Dict.)* Vol. II, p. 569. Zahrah, abū-, *al-Shāfi'ī* (Dār al-Fikr al-'Arabī, 1948) p. 14 for biography, p. 90 for differences with others and p. 143 for the legal system. Compare Yāqūt, ibn- 'Abdallāh, *Irshād al-Arīb ilā Ma'rifat al-Adīb* (Luzac, 1907) Vol. IV, pp. 367-398.

139. Khaddūrī, Ch. IV, Shāfi'ī, *(Islamic Jurisprudence)*, pp. 28-40.

(d) Analogy, or "al-qiyās" was the fourth of the "uṣūl al-fiqh." Although al-Shāfi'ī did not permit the forms of reasoning employed by some of the other jurists,[140] he did honor analogy. The Qur'ān for instance prescribes dire punishment for violent conduct, "Except for those who repent before they fall into your power; in that case know that Allāh is oft-forgiving, most merciful."[141] By analogy, punishment for other acts can also be remitted, provided there is repentance.

The Prophet was said to have forbidden the cutting off of thieves' hands during a raid, and by analogy the jurists approved of waiving penalties in enemy territory, fearing that punishments might induce the guilty persons to join the enemy.[142]

Toward the end of his life al-Shāfi'ī emphasized the importance of the Qur'ān and the sunnah, depending less and less upon consensus of opinion and analogy. He was a great scholar, whose code is the most generally accepted system in Lower Egypt, Syria, Southern India, Malaya and Indonesia. This code has been compiled in a large volume known as *Kitāb al-Umm.*[143]

4. The Ḥanbalī code was instituted by Aḥmad ibn-Ḥanbal, the last of the four founders of the generally accepted schools of legal thought.[144] Born either at Marw or Baghdād in 780 and a pupil of al-Shāfi'ī, he was famous for his collection of thirty thousand traditions, throwing light on legal matters, entitled *al-Musnad.* Even to a greater extent than al-Shāfi'ī, he held that legal decisions must be based upon the Qur'ān and the things said and done by the Prophet himself, rather than by his Companions and followers.

During the period when the son and grandson of Hārūn al-Rashīd were trying to introduce scientific and heretical ideas, ibn-Ḥanbal was the champion of orthodoxy at Baghdād. When he was put in chains by the Caliph al-Ma'mūn and later scourged by al-Mu'taṣim, the populace hailed him as a hero and a saint. The biographer ibn-Khallikān gives the following account of ibn-Ḥanbal and the troubled times in which he lived.

> In the year 220 (835 A.D.) some time between the 20th and 30th of Ramaḍān, he was required to declare that the

140. Personal opinion, *al-ra'y,* also *al-istiḥsān, al-istiṣlāḥ,* etc. See Maḥmaṣānī, pp. 27, 84-90.

141. Sūrah V, verses 36, 37.

142. Maḥmaṣānī, p. 153.

143. See Appendix III for the table of contents of *Kitāb al-Umm.*

144. Khaldūn (Quatremère) Part II, p. 400; (Rosenthal) Vol. II, p. 456. See also Patton, W. M., *Aḥmad ibn-Ḥanbal and the Miḥnā* (Brill, 1879).

> Koran was created, but would not, and although beaten and imprisoned, he persisted in his refusal. He was a handsome man of middle size, having his hair dyed of a light red colour with hinna and a few black hairs appearing in his (white) beard. He taught traditions to a number of eminent doctors, among whom were Muhammed al-Bokhari and Muslim ibn-al-Hajjaj.[145]
>
> It was estimated that the number of men present at his funeral was eight hundred thousand, and of women sixty thousand.[146]

Even though these statistics may be exaggerated, ibn-Ḥanbal was remembered with affection after he died in 855. Because, however, his legal doctrines were those of a conservative theologian rather than of a practical judge, his code is only employed in the modern world by the Wahhābī tribesmen of Arabia and other subjects of the Su'ūdī kingdom.

Such are the four officially recognized codes studied by students of the orthodox Sunnite law. Every Sunnite Muslim is expected to choose one of them as the system determining his legal status. Although it is possible to change from one code to another, children are accustomed to remain attached to the code of their fathers.

By the end of the ninth century these legal systems had become so well established, that new ideas were frowned upon and progress came to an end.[147] The authorities felt that further use of "al-ijtihād," or individual reasoning and deduction, might lead to abuse. Accordingly, for a number of centuries such changes as occurred were only in connection with matters of minor importance. Finally, legal study became so completely based upon the theories and decisions of the forefathers, that it was said, "The door of al-ijtihād is closed."

Jurisprudence and understanding the law depend upon a thorough knowledge of the Qur'ān and the Arabic language in which it is written, as well as upon mastery of at least one of the four great codes, with the traditions upon which the legal principles are based. Thus the law is one of the most difficult subjects of the curriculum, demanding acquaintance with technical details, as well as with a number of prerequisite courses.

145. Al-Bukhārī and Muslim ibn-al-Ḥajjāj have already been mentioned in connection with traditions.

146. Quoted from Khallikān *(Biog. Dict.)* Vol. I, pp. 44, 45.

147. Khaddūrī, p. 73.

In order to appreciate what a comprehensive subject the law is, a person knowing Arabic should look through a great text like *Kitāb al-Umm*, which contains the teachings of al-Shāfi'ī as compiled by his followers. At least half a page, but more often many pages, are devoted to traditions throwing light upon the legal point under discussion. Every tradition has a long list of the persons passing down the saying from the Prophet's time to later generations. After these traditions have been quoted, the jurist's own decision is given. These legal decisions deal with every phase of medieval life with an astonishing amount of detail. They are classified in a way similar to the classification of the traditions in the great collections, such as those of al-Bukhārī and Muslim. For persons unable to read Arabic, Appendix III at the back of the book gives the table of contents of *Kitāb al-Umm* with the titles translated into English.

Although most of the differences between the four authorized codes are too technical to be easily understood, the following examples illustrate in a simple way what some of the variations are like.

> According to al-Shāfi'ī and Aḥmad (ibn-Ḥanbal), if two co-proprietors wish to sell their two portions together, a purchaser has the right to buy either half by itself, or both portions together. According to Mālik and abū-Ḥanīfah the purchaser in a case of this sort does not have the right to buy one half portion of the two for sale, at the exclusion of the other half. He must either purchase both parts together or else relinquish both of them.[148]

A second example relates to the indemnity due to a Christian or Jew. According to abū-Ḥanīfah it should be equal to that of a Muslim. Mālik and ibn-Ḥanbal, on the other hand, stipulate that the blood money due a Christian or Jew should be half of that granted to a Muslim, while al-Shāfi'ī rules that it should be a third.[149] Another illustration is connected with the ownership of property. The Ḥanafī code assumes that when there is a dispute about the ownership of property, a person not actually in possession has the preferential right to prove his legal title. The Mālikī and Shāfi'ī codes hold that precedence must be given to the person actually in possession of the property, while there is uncertainty about the point of view of the Ḥanbalī code.[150]

148. Quoted from Sha'rānī, p. 361.
149. Maḥmaṣānī, p. 114.
150. *Ibid.*, p. 172.

Differences related to the rules of punishment are good examples of these legal inconsistencies. Abū-Ḥanīfah and al-Shāfi'ī require a culprit to be standing when he is beaten. Mālik allows him to sit down, while ibn-Ḥanbal is ambiguous. At the time when the culprit is being flogged, ibn-Ḥanbal allows him to wear one, or even two shirts. Mālik rules that for all offenses the clothing must be removed from the part of the body to be struck. Al-Shāfi'ī and abū-Ḥanīfah agree with Mālik except, that when the crime is merely a case of slander, the culprit may wear a garment over the part of his body to be beaten.[151]

Both ibn-Ḥanbal and abū-Ḥanīfah allow the blows to be applied to all parts of the body except the face, head and sex organs. Al-Shāfi'ī does not permit blows on places where harm might occur, with injury to the internal organs. Mālik limits flogging to parts of the back. He also holds that all cases should be punished with equally severe beatings. Abū-Ḥanīfah, on the other hand, rules that flogging should be vigorous for major offenses, somewhat milder for drunkenness and still less severe for slander. Al-Shāfi'ī offers a variation by ruling that blows for adultery should be heavier than those for slander and those for slander more vigorous than blows for drinking liquor.

As the Shī'ite law differed from that of the Sunnites and the four Sunnite codes themselves contained such detailed variations, one can easily realize why a normal student attempted to master only one, rather than a number of the legal systems. In spite of its difficulties, however, medieval law continued to meet most of the judicial requirements of Islām and to be a leading subject of the curriculum, until European innovations found their way into the Muslim world.

Because at the present time the Muslim law cannot deal with railroads and steamships, motor cars and aeroplanes, the telephone and radio, banking and insurance, stocks and bonds, labor, industry and other developments, most of the Muslim countries have established modern law schools and adopted up-to-date codes of military, penal, industrial and commercial law. Thus the Sharī'ah and the legal studies attached to it are chiefly important in the modern world in conection with marriage, divorce, inheritance, the pious foundations and religion.[152]

151. For this paragraph and the one which follows, see Sha'rānī, pp. 542, 543.

152. Refer to Khaddūrī, Chap. VI & VIII. For the modern changes in the Sharī'ah itself, see articles by J. N. D. Anderson in *The Muslim World,* Oct. 1950 to October 1952.

There is an old saying that "Jesus will descend to earth at which time the legal principles will once more be revealed, for Allāh by the voice of the Angel Gabriel will teach Jesus the law of Muhammad."[153]

A tradition like this makes one realize how impossible it is to separate law from theology. While the scholars were busying themselves with legal matters, they also turned their attention to questions of a more metaphysical nature. Even though their theology was speculative and pedantic, it was just as popular in medieval Islām as scholasticism was in Europe.

Theology

Theology as a science[154] did not originate with the Prophet, because the Qur'ān was a spiritual revelation rather than an integrated system of dogma, while Muḥammad was a prophet rather than a theologian. As al-Ash'arī said, "No question was dealt with in a specific way by the Book and the sunnah, because analysis of intellectual questions did not occur during the days of the Prophet, may Allāh bless him and his family and give them peace."[155]

The Qur'ān condemned "Those who divide their religion, becoming partisans, each party rejoicing in what was its own."[156] Unfortunately, however, it was not long before the faith of the Prophet became a complicated system of dogma, while so many sects developed that it required large volumes to describe them.[157]

One of the first questions to be discussed was connected with the Prophet's successor, who was the ruler of the Muslim theocracy. If the caliph is a bad man, will Allāh condemn him or, in spite of his sins, will Allāh accept him as a believer?[158]

One party called "al-Khawārij" formulated the doctrine that every Muslim, even the caliph, would go to hell if he should sin and fail to repent. Numerous opponents objected to this extreme

153. Sha'rānī, p. 33.

154. In Arabic, theology is the science of *al-kalām* (the word), *al-tawḥīd* (oneness), or *uṣūl al-dīn* (origins of the religion).

155. Translated from Ash'arī, al-, *The Theology of al-Ash'arī* Edit. R. J. McCarthy (Impr. Catholique, Beirut, 1953) p. 94 (Arab.) Compare p. 129 (English.)

156. Sūrah XXX, verse 32.

157. Examples are Shahrastānī, al-, *Kitāb al-Milal wa'l-Niḥal* and Baghdādī, al-, *Moslem Schisms and Sects,* Trans. Kate C. Seelye (Columbia Univ. Press, 1920); Halkin (Tel-Aviv 1935).

158. Consult Ḥittī *(Arabs)* pp. 179-182. Khaldūn (Quatremère) Part III, pp. 27-43; (Rosenthal) Vol. III, pp. 34-75.

view, developing a more moderate dogma of their own. The members of this group were called "al-Murji'ah."[159] Instead of condemning the caliph they felt that they should obey him, postponing a decision about his character until the Day of Judgment, when Allāh himself would decide whether the caliph should go to heaven or hell.

They, moreover, formed the dogma that nothing can save except faith, which is so important that even if a believer should sin, he would not remain in hell. They held that faith was more essential than good works, emphasizing the mercy of Allāh and claiming that no Muslim will be eternally damned.

Some of the caliphs, however, as well as many less conspicuous believers, led such evil lives that it seemed unreasonable for them to escape without any punishment. This raised the question,—is there temporary punishment for a man who believes, but at the same time sins? Although numerous Muslim scholars suggested solutions to this problem, they did not develop a doctrine as definite as the Catholic dogma of purgatory.

One of the greatest of the Murji'ah was the famous jurist abū-Ḥanīfah. He emphasized the fact that faith should be not merely a matter of the lips, but also of the heart, accompanied by good works. In a similar way the philosopher of history, ibn-Khaldūn, explained that belief in the oneness of Allāh demands a blending of God's qualities in the soul, stimulating an observance of the Qur'ānic ordinances, and faith in the tenets of Islām.[160]

Another problem occupying the minds of the Muslim scholars was the conflict between predestination and freedom of the will. The following examples illustrate how the Qur'ān itself can be used to support both sides of the dispute. First there are some verses favoring predestination.

> No blow strikes on earth or in your souls, unless it is in a book before we cause it to come to pass. (Sūrah LVII, verse 22.) I (Allāh) will mislead them and I will create in them false desires. (Sūrah IV, verse 119.)
>
> He whom Allāh wishes to guide, He will open his breast to Islām, and he whom He wishes to let go astray, He will make his breast closed and forbidding. (Sūrah VI, verse 125.)
>
> No soul can believe except by Allāh's will. (Sūrah X, verse 100.)

159. Shahrastānī, pp. 103, 108. Macdonald *(Dev. Muslim)* pp. 123-126.
160. Khaldūn (Quatremère) Part III, p. 33; (Rosenthal) Vol. III, p. 39.

> You do not will, except as Allāh wills. (Sūrah LXXVI, verse 30.)

Then there are examples of the kind of verses which can be used to prove freedom of the will.

> Whatever good befalls thee is from Allāh and whatever evil befalls thee is from thyself. (Sūrah IV, verse 79.) We test thee by evil and by good, by way of trial. (Sūrah XXI, verse 35.) That each soul may find the reward of what is earned and none of them be wronged. (Sūrah XLV, verse 22.) Those who believe and do righteous deeds, their Lord will cause them to enter into His mercy. (Sūrah XLV, verse 30.) The truth is from your Lord, let him who will, believe and let him, so wishing, reject it. (Sūrah XVIII, verse 29.)

The school of thought upholding predestination was called "al-Jabrīyah," whereas "al-Qadarīyah" supported freedom of the will.[161]

At first the theologians discussed their problems and supported their arguments by quoting verses of the Qur'ān and the sayings of the Prophet.[162] The Umayyad Caliphs at Damascus discouraged theological discussions, preferring to take for granted the doctrine of predestination, so as to make their subjects think that misfortunes were due to God's decree rather than to bad government. On the other hand, they did allow the Muslim scholars to meet with John of Damascus and other Christian theologians, who interested their Muslim associates in the dogmatic controversies of the Christian sects. During this early period individual scholars interpreted the passages of the Qur'ān in conflicting ways, theology not yet being systematic in its development.

As early as the first half of the eighth century, however, there appeared an important group of rationalistic scholars, who used reason and logic to prove their doctrines. It was because of their skill in argument that the orthodox scholars were obliged to defend themselves by forming a dogmatic system of their own.

This new group of scholars, who were called "al-Mu'tazilah,"[163]

161. *Jabrīyah* is derived from *al-jabr* or compulsion; *Qadarīyah* from *al-qadar* or power. See Shahrastānī, p. 59; Ash'arī, al-, *Al-Ibānah 'an Uṣūl al-Diyānah,* Trans. W. C. Klein (Amer. Oriental Soc., 1940), p. 113.

162. Qanawātī, M. M. & L. Gardet, *Introduction à la Théologie Musulmane* (Librarie Philosophique J. Vrin, 1948), p. 30.

163. Some authorities name Wāṣil ibn-'Aṭā' as the originator of the Mu'tazilī movement, but Nadīm (Beatty MS.) p. 107 names 'Amr ibn-'Ubayd. For the story of the founding of the movement, see Nicholson *(Lit. Hist.)* pp. 222, 223. See also Shahrastānī, pp. 29-31; Ash'arī *(Ibānah)* pp. 15-24. Nādir, Albert Naṣrī, *Le System Philosophique des Mu'tazila* (Les Lettres Orientales, Beirut, 1956).

originated at al-Baṣrah, but soon became active at Baghdād. Although Hārūn al-Rashīd objected to some of their ideas, his three successors adopted certain of their tenets as their official dogmas.

Because the caliphs were fostering Greek science at the same time that they were supporting this new movement, it is not surprising that the scholars of al-Mu'tazilah were influenced by philosophical ideas. Thus they used Aristotle's "Analytics" and methods of logic to carry on discussions about metaphysical questions. It was this form of dialectic which was called "al-kalām," the term eventually used for theology.

The following doctrines were some of the important tenets of al-Mu'tazilah. Allāh is completely spiritual and transcendent above matter. He cannot have separate attributes like knowledge, power, speech, hearing and seeing, because they would be contrary to his oneness, conceived of in anthropomorphic or human terms.[164]

God's justice, moreover, makes it impossible for him, first to foreordain that a man should sin and, later, to send the same man to hell because he did sin. Thus man must possess freedom of the will. Because of these two dogmas the scholars of al-Mu'tazilah were called the "People of Justness and Oneness."[165]

A third doctrine was the belief that the Qur'ān was created, it not being consistent with the oneness of Allāh to suppose that the Qur'ān was, like God himself, an uncreated existence. Thus although members of al-Mu'tazilah believed that Allāh inspired the Prophet Muḥammad, giving him revealed knowledge, they insisted that instead of being the pre-existent speech of Allāh, the Qur'ān was one of God's finite creations.[166]

In 833 the Caliph al-Ma'mūn became so interested in this dogma of the creation of the Qur'ān that he established an inquisition,[167] so as to oblige the jurists and theologians to accept the doctrine. The Caliphs al-Mu'taṣim and al-Wāthiq maintained the persecution, but al-Mutawakkil, who ruled from 847 to 861, ordered a return to orthodoxy. Because the basis of belief and

164. See Qur'ān, Sūrah II, verse 255 and LIX—22 for knowledge; II—255 and LIX—23 for power; X—99,100 and LXXXI—29 for will; VI—115 and XXVII—62 for hearing; LIV—14 for seeing; II—117 for speaking. The Arabic for attributes is *al-ṣifāt*.

165. *Ahl al-'Adl wa'l-Tawḥīd*.

166. Bouman, Johan, *Le Conflit autour du Coran et la Solution d'al-Baqillānī* (Van Campen, Amsterdam, 1959).

167. *Al-Miḥnah*.

behavior in Islām is faith in the Qur'ān as the uncreated, pre-existent speech of Allāh, this doctrine of the creation of the Qur'ān stirred up a great deal of bitterness among the orthodox scholars, whose famous champion was Aḥmad ibn-Ḥanbal, already mentioned in connection with the four Sunnite codes of law.

A fourth doctrine of al-Mu'tazilah was that faith not only involves acceptance of belief, but also righteous living with avoidance of major sins. Not only infidels but also Muslim sinners must go to hell, but the punishment of a believer is less severe than that of an infidel. There were other less important doctrines, not so generally accepted as to require mention in this brief account.

These rationalistic ideas of al-Mu'tazilah, accompanying the introduction of Greek science during the ninth century, resulted in a great deal of free thought and agnosticism. The scholars were confused by conflicting beliefs, while the common people became emotionally aroused by doctrines threatening to undermine their faith.

It was, therefore, a great relief when a famous scholar named al-Ash'arī[168] came to the rescue with a system of belief acceptable to the majority of the people. He was especially well fitted for this task, as he was a member of al-Mu'tazilah before he became converted to the orthodox point of view.

Al-Ash'arī was born about 874 at al-Baṣrah, where he grew up as a disciple of the great scholar of al-Mu'tazilah known as al-Jubbā'ī.[169] Some time after his master died about 915, he lost faith in the doctrines of al-Mu'tazilah, renouncing them in a public way. Until he himself died about 936, he was able to exert a great influence, because he won so many friends by his reasonableness and avoidance of extremes. Appendix IV at the back of the book gives a summary of his beliefs, which formed the basis of orthodox theological instruction, not only in medieval times, but also during the centuries which followed.

It was al-Ash'arī who made *al-kalām* a legitimate science for the orthodox scholars to study. This term meaning "speech"[170] was originally used for the Qur'ān, but was later applied to the dialectic indulged in by the rationalistic scholars. Before the time

168. Abū-al-Ḥasan 'Alī ibn-Ismā'īl al-Ash'arī, see Khallikān *(Biog. Dict.)* Vol. II, p. 227; Nicholson, pp. 377-379; Ash'arī *(Ibānah)* p. 25 ff., *(Theology)* p. 150 ff.

169 Abū-'Alī Muḥammad al-Jubbā'ī, see Khallikān *(Biog. Dict.)* Vol. II, pp. 669, 670.

170. *Enc. of Islam,* Vol. II, p. 670.

of al-Ash'arī it was not considered fitting for an orthodox Muslim to argue with scholars of al-Mu'tazilah and with free thinkers, or to seek the truth by means of reason. The only legitimate way to find the truth was by studying the Qur'ān and the traditions. Even logic[171] was outlawed, because it seemed to depend upon reason rather than revelation.

Al-Ash'arī described this conservative point of view when he wrote, "A group of men have made ignorance their capital. Finding reasoning and inquiry into religious belief too burdensome, they incline towards the easy way of servile sectarianism."[172]

Al-Ash'arī was not content merely to criticize the old bigotry; he took active steps to introduce new methods of his own. With the help of some of his contemporaries he started to use logic and the art of debate, so as to refute the rationalistic scholars by means of their own practices. This change of method made the art of disputation acceptable as one of the religious sciences. Thus Islām developed a system of theology similar to the scholasticism of Europe.

Ibn-Khaldūn says that this theology is a "Science, which by means of intellectual proofs, confirms doctrines depending upon faith and refutes the dogmatic innovations of scholars deviating from the beliefs of the original Muslims."[173]

Thus al-Ash'arī and his associates used reason, not to form new doctrines but to defend the old ones. It was in this way that they were able to enjoy the confidence of the conservatives, in spite of the fact that they used radical methods. The aim of al-Ash'arī was to accomplish a compromise between the followers of ibn-Ḥanbal and al-Mu'tazilah. In connection, therefore, with doctrines like freedom of the will, the attributes, the vision of God, the throne of God, the creation of the Qur'ān, anthropomorphic conceptions of God, damnation of a believer, intercession of the Prophet and the legitimacy of the caliphs, al-Ash'arī tried to find compromises for mutual understanding.

The many compositions of al-Ash'arī[174] prove the masterful way in which he formed his doctrinal system. The following examples suggest a few of the problems discussed by him and his disciples.

In the first place, there is the conception of Allāh as oneness,

171. *Al-manṭiq.*
172. Ash'arī *(Theology)* p. 120. "Servile sectarianism" is *al-taqlīd.*
173. Khaldūn (Quatremère) Part III, p. 27; (Rosenthal) Vol. III, p. 34.
174. Ash'arī *(Theology)* pp. 211-230; *(Ibānah)* pp. 29, 30.

because of his being the original creator. Everything must have a cause and there must be a causer of causes. This initiator of causes is God. The Muslim theologians refuted the idea of Aristotle that the finite world is eternal. They taught instead that the atoms and accidents composing phenomena are constantly perishing and being generated. This implies creation and, if there is creation, there must be a creator. Everything temporal must have a cause. The world is temporal, therefore the world itself must have a cause.[175]

Even man himself cannot exist without a creator.

> The proof of this is that the completely mature man was originally semen, then a clot, then a small lump, then flesh and bone and blood. Now we know very well that he did not translate himself from state to state . . . His translation from state to state without a translator and governor is impossible.[176]

After confirming their faith that Allāh was the first cause, the theologians dealt with another truth. God the Creator is unlike the creatures He creates. As the Qur'ān says, "There is nothing like Him" and "No one is His equal."[177]

Certain verses of the Qur'ān, however, suggest that Allāh has human characteristics. Thus we read, "The Merciful is established on the throne." "The face of thy Lord will abide full of majesty." "I have created with my hands." and "It floats under Our eyes."[178]

The theologians attached to al-Ash'arī explained such verses as the jurist Mālik explained them. Instead of arguing about the throne and eyes and hands of Allāh, they said that such things must be accepted "without asking how."[179]

Ibn-Khaldūn throws light on this attitude of mind when he says that God has imparted to a man only a limited portion of knowledge. A human being, therefore, cannot understand the universe with his finite mind any better than he can weigh a mountain with scales made for measuring gold. Man must have faith in the truths revealed by Allāh.[180]

Mention has already been made of the verses of the Qur'ān

175. Khaldūn (Quatremère) Part III, pp. 27-30; (Rosenthal) Vol. III, pp. 34-38.

176. Ash'arī *(Theology)* p. 6 ff. See also *Muslim World,* Vol. xlvii, No. 2, pp. 136, 139, 141.

177. Sūrah XLII, verse 11; CXII, verse 4.

178. Sūrah XX, verse 5; LV, verse 27; XXXVIII, verse 75; LIV, verse 14.

179. *Bilā kayfa.*

180. Khaldūn (Quatremère) Part III, p. 30; (Rosenthal) Vol. III. p. 38.

which speak of the divine attributes. For al-Ash'arī there were seven of these *ṣifāt* or attributes: life, knowledge, power, will, hearing, seeing and speech. But if Allāh possessed these seven attributes, how could He be one? This problem provided the Muslim theologians with a metaphysical enigma similar to the Christian mystery of the Trinity. The orthodox acceptance of the attributes was opposed to the position of al-Mu'tazilah, who as has already been explained denied the existence of the attributes along with bodily forms of God.[181]

At the same time that the theologians were discussing the oneness and character of Allāh, they were keeping alive the old controversy as to whether there was predestination or freedom of the will. The Mu'tazilah continued to uphold man's freedom to choose for himself and to maintain that Allāh was too just to foreordain first sin and then its punishment. They persisted in arguing that it is man himself who by free choice disobeys God, incurring punishment because of this disobedience.

The position of al-Ash'arī in connection with this controversy is a compromise based on subtle reasoning. According to him, although everything is foreordained by Allāh, man possesses the ability to acquire predestined actions, without affecting the actions themselves.[182]

When discussing the other dispute, as to whether the Qur'ān is created or uncreated, al-Ash'arī wrote

> Why do you hold that God has ever been speaking and that the word of God is uncreated? We hold this because God has said 'When we will a thing our only utterance is that we say to it 'BE' and it is.'[183] So if the Qur'ān had been created, God would have said to it 'BE.' But the Qur'ān is His speech, and it is impossible that His speech should be spoken to.[184]

Such were some of the more important doctrines of al-Ash'arī, who was the most influential of the orthodox theologians of his period. His method of using logic and dialectic to combat the free thinkers was employed by many other scholars throughout the Muslim world. Thus al-Ṭahāwī[185] developed theology in Egypt,

181. Ash'arī *(Theology)* pp. 12-33.
182. Nicholson *(Lit. Hist.)* p. 379. Ash'arī *(Theology)* pp. 33-44..
183. Qur'ān, Sūrah II, verse 117.
184. Ash'arī *(Theology)* p. 20. See also the Arabic, p. 15.
185. Abū-Ja'far Aḥmad al-Ṭaḥāwī, 854-933, an Egyptian jurist; see Nadīm, p. 207; Khallikān *(Biog. Dict.)* Vol. I, pp. 51, 52.

while al-Māturīdī[186] made scholastic discussions popular in far away Samarqand. Several centuries later the dramatic leader named ibn-Tūmart[187] carried this type of theological reasoning to North Africa and from there it crossed to Spain.

One of the principal disciples of al-Ash'arī was al-Bāqillānī,[188] who introduced a theory of monads into orthodox Islām. By creating and destroying the monads Allāh produces everything in the world. If for example one writes a letter, it is God who by means of his monads gives the will to write, the power to write, the motion of writing, the paper and the pen. Thus an atomic theory entered into Muslim thought.

So many other scholars gave lectures and wrote books about theological questions, that it is impossible in this brief account to discuss their conflicting ideas, or even to mention their names.[189] As, however, both Niẓām-al-Mulk and Saladin[190] encouraged the theology of al-Ash'arī in the many colleges which they founded, theological courses after their time were based largely on the system of al-Ash'arī.

Although dry discussions about metaphysical questions provided an intellectual pastime for the scholars, they did not meet the emotional needs of the people as a whole. This was especially true during a period when governments were despotic, the officials often corrupt and cruel, slavery so common that social morality was at a low ebb, the populations ravaged by epidemics and life upset by constant fighting. People craved spiritual help, hoping that their suffering would be rewarded by the joys of heaven.

As the result of these conditions, another form of religious activity developed side by side with theology. This was the *Ṣūfī* movement, which comprised both asceticism and mysticism.[191] Although its doctrines were often included in the medieval curriculum, the subject was supplementary to theology and therefore need be mentioned only briefly.[192]

186. Abū-Manṣūr Muḥammad al-Māturidī (Māṭaridī), died 944; see Tritton, A. S., *(Muslim Theology)* (Luzac, 1947), pp. 174-176; Ash'arī *(Ibānah)* p. 37.

187. Muḥammad ibn-Tūmart declared himself as al-Mahdī, 1121, founding the Muwaḥḥid Dynasty.

188. Abū-Bakr Muḥammad al-Bāqillānī of al-Baṣrah became a leading disciple of al-Ash'arī. He died at Baghdād 1013. See Khallikān *(Biog. Dict.)* Vol. II, p. 671; Tritton *(Muslim Theol.)* pp. 179-183.

189. See Qanawātī, pp. 60-67, and for translations of well known creeds, Macdonald *(Dev. Muslim)* pp. 293-351.

190. Refer to the section on "The College".

191. The term *Ṣūfī* may have come from the Greek *sophos,* but more likely from the *ṣūf* or wool worn by the ascetic. Numerous books about the *Ṣūfī* movement are included in the bibliography.

192. The system of doctrines and practices was called *al-taṣawwuf.*

Even as early as the eighth century pioneer ascetics tried to avoid the evils of the world and to gain entrance to paradise, by means of austerity and pious living. At first the devotee was a simple ascetic,[193] living a life of renunciation without any attempt to form theological doctrines of his own. In the course of time, however, some of the Ṣūfīs[194] developed their own dogmatic interpretation of religion, frequently influenced by Neo-Platonism. They also evolved a system of stations, to help the Ṣūfī rise from material to spiritual things, until finally by ecstatic union he could become one with Allāh.

Many of the Ṣūfīs were normal men and women, devoting themselves to pious practices in an unassuming way. Most of them were greatly revered by the common people, while a few like al-Ḥallāj[195] suffered dramatic martyrdom. Others like al-Junayd[196] were scholars, who turned mysticism into an intellectual system. As some of these Ṣūfīs indulged in strange practices and made extreme statements, the orthodox theologians felt obliged to condemn them. Al-Junayd, therefore, was so afraid of the hostility of the orthodox scholars, that he never dared to issue his books to the public, requesting his disciples to bury them when he died.

Finally a great scholar known as al-Ghazzālī[197] appeared to make the more reasonable ideas of the Ṣūfīs acceptable. He was a saint, who, like Francis of Assisi, vitalized the dry formulas of medieval thought with a touch of poetry and mysticism, changing theology from the ivory tower speculation of the scholars into a living faith for the masses. Unlike Saint Francis he did not found a brotherhood, but was a great theologian and philosopher, his profilic works being still studied throughout the Muslim world.

The life of al-Ghazzālī was an epic of religious experience. He was born at Ṭūs in 1058, three years after the Saljūq Turks gained control of the Islamic empire and turned the 'Abbāsid Caliph into a puppet, deprived of all power. His youth coincided with the period when William the Conqueror was establishing his rule in England and Niẓām-al-Mulk was serving as the great vizier of the Saljūq sultāns. He completed his primary education

193. The ascetic was *al-zāhid.*

194. The Arabic plural is *al-ṣuffīyah, ahl al-ṣuffah,* or *al-ṣūfīyūn.*

195. Ḥusayn ibn-Manṣūr al-Ḥallāj, executed at Baghdād 922. See Massignon, Louis, *Al-Hallaj, Martyr Mystique de l'Islam* (Geuthner, 1922).

196. Abū-al-Qāsim al-Junayd, died 910. See Nadīm, p. 186; Khallikān *(Biog. Dict.)* Vol. I, p. 338.

197. Abū-Ḥāmid Muḥammad al-Ghazzālī, called Ḥujjat al-Islām. His name is often written al-Ghazālī. See Khallikān *(Biog. Dict.)* Vol. I, p. 80; Vol. II, p. 621. Also Watt, W. M., *The Faith and Practice of al-Ghazālī,* (Allen & Unwin, 1953), pp. 11-85.

in his native town, after which he went to the nearby city of Naysābūr, at that time one of the intellectual centers of Islām. He studied with a great scholar[198] until this teacher died in 1085, ten years before the beginning of the First Crusade. He once said about himself, "To thirst after a comprehension of things as they really are was my habit and custom from a very early age."[199] Accordingly, he not only mastered the conventional studies connected with language, law and theology, but also delved into the philosophical systems of his time. Distressed by the existence of conflicting sects and contradictory theories, and refusing to be satisfied with the doctrines of his elders, he tried to find the truth by means of personal study and experience.

When his master died at Naysābūr, al-Ghazzālī became attached to Niẓām-al-Mulk, who in 1091 appointed him to teach in the Niẓāmīyah College at Baghdād. While there, al-Ghazzālī completed his book entitled *Destruction of the Philosophers,*[200] an analysis and critique of the subtleties of the Greek and Arab metaphysicians. In 1095 he had what was probably a nervous breakdown, due largely to his loss of faith and fear of hell. He left his enviable position at Baghdād to become an ascetic, wandering about in search of truth. He visited Damascus, Jerusalem, Makkah, al-Madīnah, Alexandria, Baghdād and Naysābūr, teaching and writing many of his greatest books,[201] at the same time indulging in mystical practices. Finally he withdrew to his native town of Ṭūs, where he died in 1111 A.D.

As a theologian al-Ghazzālī believed that the human soul belongs to the spiritual rather than the material world. This is confirmed by the Qur'ān when it says that Allāh breathed into man His spirit.[202] This spirit contains a spark of divinity and therefore seeks to return to its source. Thus it is natural for a Ṣūfī to strive to reach Allāh by means of mysticism.

Al-Ghazzālī divided the sciences into different groups, separating the systems relying on reason from those based on revelation.[203] By using Aristotelian logic he further developed the teaching of

198. Abū-al-Ma'ālī 'Abd-al-Malik al-Juwaynī, Imām al-Ḥaramayn, see Khallikān *(Biog. Dict.)* Vol. II, p. 120.

199. Ghazzālī, al-, *The Faith and Practice of al-Ghazālī,* with translation from *Al-Munqidh min al-Ḍalāl,* p. 21.

200. *Tahāfut al-Falāsifah.*

201. Among these books was his famous *Iḥyā' 'Ulūm al-Dīn.*

202. Sūrah XV, verse 29 and XXXVIII, verse 72.

203. See Ghazzālī, al-, *Ih'ya Ouloūm ed-Dīn,* Edit. G. H. Bousquet (Max Besson, 1955), pp. 23, 24, 26, 30 and Anawātī, p. 116.

al-Ash'arī, joining Greek techniques with Muslim doctrines. He accepted such of the Neo-Platonic dogmas as were in accord with Islām, but exposed those which were opposed to the true faith. As a mystic he held that Allāh gives light directly to the human heart. Revelation, therefore, cannot be explained merely in terms of academic definitions and theological dogmas; it must also be understood by means of spiritual communion with God.

He was too practical to expect the ordinary believer to understand theology, which was chiefly useful for defense of the established faith. Reserving difficult problems for the scholars, he emphasized for the masses the importance of ethical living and good works. At the same time he revived a fear of hell, an emphasis upon repentance and an acknowledgment of God's great love. In his book *The Beginning of Guidance*[204] he explains how a Muslim can obey the Qur'ānic ordinances and the precedents of the Prophet.

The ethics of al-Ghazzālī were a blending of Muslim, Greek and Ṣūfī ideas, that is of revelation, reason and divine guidance. He emphasized the importance of the Golden Mean and was influenced both by Aristotle and Plato. In one section of his great work entitled *Ihyā' 'Ulūm al-Dīn* he discusses spiritual endeavor and self-discipline. He speaks about vices such as loose speaking, anger and envy, worldliness and stinginess, social pride and hypocrisy, conceit and deception. This discussion is followed by constructive suggestions for pious living and contemplation of life hereafter. One example must suffice to illustrate the kind of ethical teaching that this book contains.

There are two remedies for pride. "One of them is extermination of its roots from their base and uprooting its trunk planted in the heart. The second is prevention of the special causes, which lead a man to exalt himself above his fellows."[205] The first remedy is made effective by the command "Know thyself and the Almighty." The second involves knowledge and good works, so as to overcome the seven causes of pride in the following way. Do not be haughty because of noble birth. Refrain from vanity because of a beautiful body, for one must realize how much urine and filth come from the body every day. Do not be conceited because of physical strength, but remember how prone man is to bodily infirmity. Realize that wealth and power bring only

204. *Bidāyat al-Hidāyah,* see Ghazzālī *(Faith and Practice)* pp. 90-130.

205. For this translation and the remainder of the paragraph, see Ghazzālī, al-, *Iḥyā' al-Ulūm* (al-Maymūnīyah Press, Cairo, 1916.)

external importance, instead of spiritual growth, and finally be sure that much learning does not produce spiritual pride, or ascetic living, hypocrisy.

In a little book entitled *O Youth*[206] there are some beautiful sentences throwing light on al-Ghazzālī's attitude towards life. He quotes a passage of the Qur'ān, "The mercy of Allāh is near to the door of good deeds,"[207] after which he makes a number of statements like the three examples which follow. "Knowledge is the tree and working is its fruit." "Knowledge without work is insanity and work without knowledge is vanity." "Goodness of conduct among men is that you do not burden people according to your own desire, but burden yourself according to their desires, so long as they do not violate the sacred law."[208]

Al-Ghazzālī wrote so many books about such a variety of subjects, that it is impossible to do justice to his work in a few pages. By encyclopaedic learning, saintly living and a mystical power of spirit he gave new meaning to theology, reviving the vigorous faith of the Prophet. Ever since his time theological courses have been based to a large extent upon his teachings, as well as on those of al-Ash'arī.

Just as the Crusades, the Mongolian invasions and centuries of Ottoman oppression brought the development of Arabic literature to a halt, these same causes resulted in a similar stagnation of theology. Even leaders like ibn-Taymīyah[209] were more reactionary than creative, while the rank and file of the scholars coming after al-Ghazzālī wrote expositions of the older books, rather than undertaking original research of their own.

It is difficult to tell where theology ends and philosophy begins. In one of his short creeds, for instance, al-Ghazzālī stated that Allāh "Is not a substance and substances do not exist in Him; and He is not an accident and accidents do not exist in Him."[210] Al-Ash'arī referred to discussions about "Motion and rest, body and accident, accidental modes and states, the atom and the leap, and the attributes of the Creator."[211]

206. See Ghazzālī, al-, *O Youth (Ayyuha'l-Walad)*, Edit. G. H. Scherer (Amer. Press, Beirut, 1933).

207. Sūrah VII, verse 56 (54).

208. Ghazzālī *(O Youth)* pp. 55, 56, 58, 68.

209. Taqī-al-Dīn Aḥmad ibn-Ṭaymīyah, born 1263, lived at Damascus, worked in Cairo, persecuted for his views, died at Damascus 1328.

210. Macdonald *(Dev. Muslim)* p. 301.

211. Ash'arī *(Theology)* p. 120. "Leap" (al-ṭafrah) is passage of a body through units of space without occupying them.

Before the time of al-Ash'arī, members of al-Mu'tazilah started to discuss many metaphysical questions, while the mystics were constantly in danger of confusing their ideas with pantheism. Many of the thinkers were puzzled by the contradiction between the Qur'ānic idea of creation, through the word of Allāh, and the Neo-Platonic theory of emanations. Thus they asked the question: is the soul of man a tenuous, corporeal substance created by Allāh, or something spiritual and immaterial resulting from emanation?

Examples of this sort make it evident that theology and philosophy often dealt with similar problems. As a rule, however, theology depended upon the revelation of the Qur'ān, whereas philosophy was based on reason, following the teachings of the Greek sages and Neo-Platonists.

Theology, therefore, became an important subject of the curriculum, while philosophy was almost always taught by private teachers, often in their own homes. Thus, although logic was included in the medieval program of studies, the more important subject of philosophy was not as a rule given an official place in the curriculum.

In spite of the fact that music[212] was studied by the scholars and favored by the Ṣūfīs, it too was not formally recognized. In the same way mathematics was regarded as a subject of secondary importance, although it was useful for calculating the division of inheritance and for fixing the times of feasts, fasts and prayers. A village boy could not always learn arithmetic at his neighborhood mosque, frequently being obliged to have special lessons with a public weigher or land measurer.[213] Even in the large colleges, the important professors did not teach subjects which had no direct connection with the revelation of Allāh. Although mathematics, astronomy and the natural sciences were dealt with by individual scholars, while medicine and pharmacy were taught in the hospitals, these subjects were not included in the generally accepted curriculum.

In medieval times the curriculum was composed of the linguistic, legal and religious studies, which have been described in the preceding pages. These were subjects of primary importance, as they are concerned with the revelations of Allāh. They not only had theoretical and spiritual value, but were also exceedingly

212. Khaldūn (Quatremère) Part II, pp. 352-361; (Rosenthal) Vol. II, pp. 395-405.

213. The mosque school was *al-kuttāb*, the public weigher *al-qabbānī* and the land measurer *al-massāḥ*.

practical, as they provided a thorough knowledge of the language, in which the revelations were imparted, and explained how the Prophet Muḥammad interpreted them. Thus the program of studies, employed by the teachers of medieval times, furnished the students with a comprehensive understanding of the Qur'ān, with its guiding principles for every phase of life during the Middle Ages.

Conclusion

As modern science and industry did not affect Islām before the nineteenth century, medieval forms of education continued to exist in the Muslim lands for an extended period of time. Although an Arabic printing press was established in Rome during the sixteenth century and another in Syria in 1698, these presses were used by Christian churchmen, rather than by Muslim scholars.

On the other hand, when Napoleon Bonaparte invaded Egypt, at the end of the eighteenth century, his French scientists opened the eyes of numerous Muslim scholars to appreciate the importance of European learning. During the nineteenth century, first Muḥammad 'Alī and later the Khedive Ismā'īl encouraged the founding of professional schools of a modern type in Egypt. The British rule in India, the French influence in North Africa and the spread of missionary schools throughout the Middle East also introduced new forms of education. The Turks, moreover, were affected by Western ideas, as many of their leading citizens visited European cities, engaging foreign tutors and governesses for their children.

In 1866 there was founded a small college which grew rapidly, becoming the American University of Beirut. Eight years later, the French Jesuit Université Saint-Joseph was also established. These two institutions of higher learning at Beirut were largely responsible for the "Arab Awakening," which occurred before the First World War.

The instituting of the French and British mandates in the Middle East, as well as the extension of colonial rule in other Muslim regions, gave further impetus to this process of modernization. Finally, the creation of independent governments produced a widespread demand for modern schools, to supplant medieval forms of education.

The first step, which almost every Muslim state has taken, upon gaining independence, has been the organizing of an extensive system of national education.[214] The new institutions are secular rather than religious, encouraging the scientific method instead of dependence upon authority. They stress the need for laboratory work and research, introducing technical courses to take the place of studies based on the Qur'ān. What is especially significant is the fact that they encourage coeducation and the training of women for all phases of modern life.

Not only are great modern universities being established in the Muslim countries, but a number of ancient institutions are being modernized. Thus al-Azhar at Cairo now has entrance requirements, formal registration, strict examinations, official diplomas, modern classrooms, improved textbooks, a central library and an organized system for appointing teachers. With handsome new halls for the academic work and over forty new buildings to house the students, al-Azhar is very different from what it used to be.[215] What is even more striking is the fact that a new law decrees the development of new colleges during the next five years. In addition to the theological, legal and liberal arts courses, there are to be colleges of medicine, engineering, agriculture and business administration.[216]

When, moreover, Morocco became independent, steps were taken to change the Qarawīyīn into a modern university. During the autumn of 1960 there were 6,325 students, 1,197 of whom were girls. A new campus is being developed, with modern classrooms and dormitories, in addition to an infirmary, dining halls, a library and athletic facilities.[217]

Numerous Muslim schools still teach the subjects of the medieval curriculum, in the same way that Christian seminaries offer courses in Hebrew, Bible exegesis and systematic theology.[218] These religious courses are needed to train mosque leaders and legal authorities. The Muslim law, however, no longer suffices for every phase of life, its usefulness being limited to cases

214. There are now large numbers of elementary schools in the cities and important villages, secondary schools in the towns and state universities in the capital cities, as well as in some of the provincial centers.

215. Dodge (*al-Azhar*), chap. VII and appendices V & VI.

216. *Majallat al-Azhar*, July, 1961. p. 215.

217. *New York Times*, Oct. 9, 1960.

218. In addition to a number of large mosque colleges in the Arab lands, like the Zaytūnah in Tunisia and al-Najaf in 'Irāq, there are also numerous smaller schools. At Qūm and Mashhed in Iran and a number of centers in the Indian subcontinent and South-East Asia, there are also institutions which still use the studies of the medieval curriculum.

connected with marriage, divorce, inheritance and the pious foundations.

Thus the Muslim education of the Middle Ages is rapidly being superseded by schools and universities, which are both modern and secular. This widespread movement is so recent that it is impossible to tell how it will affect the cultural and social life of Islām.

It is clear, however, that in this age of chaotic change, when members of the rising generation are confused by bewildering doubts, the reformers must not neglect the basic principles of medieval education, which were a search for spiritual truth and faith in the reality of Allāh.

Appendix I

System of Transliteration from Arabic to English

Bā	b	Zayn	z	Fā	f
Tā	t	Sīn	s	Qāf	
Thā	th	Shīn	sh	Kāf	k
Jīm	j	Ṣāḍ	s	Lām	l
Ḥā	h	Ḍāḍ	ḍ	Mīm	m
Khā	kh	Ṭā	t	Nūn	n
Dāl	d	Ẓā	ẓ	Hā	h
Dhāl	dh	‘Ayn		Wāw	w
Rā	r	Ghayn	gh	Yā	y

Alif as a long vowel or maqṣūrah, ā

Vowels and Diphthongs.

Fatḥah	(short)	a,	(long)	a
Kasrah	”	i,	”	ı
Ḍammah	”	u,	”	u
	Fatḥah – Wāw		aw	
	” Yā		ay	

Shaddah is indicated by a doubling of the consonant, but with Kasrah – Yā is written as in Ismā‘īlīyah.

The definite article is only written with a capital at the beginning of a sentence.

The nisbah is written ī.

Final Hā is written with an – h – rather than – t –, except when it is in construct state.

Unless they occur at the beginning of the sentence, names like *abū* and *ibn* are written with small letters. They are also connected by hyphens with the names which follow them.

Appendix II

Traditions of the Prophet Muḥammad. Contents of "al-Ṣaḥīḥ" of al-Bukharī

Title of the chapter (al-kitāb) given in English and Arabic transliteration[1]	*Number of pages of Arabic printing*
How the revelation began (kayf kān bad' al-waḥī)	6
Faith (al-īmān)	17
Knowledge (al-'ilm)	23
Ritual washing (al-wuḍū')	26
Washing (al-ghasl), bathing, perfuming and details for washing	9
Menstruation (al-ḥayḍ), its purification	9
Purification with sand (al-tayammum), when water is lacking	6
Prayer (al-ṣalāt),[2] with details for dress, floor matting, the direction to face in prayer, unusual places, the building and use of mosques	42
Times of prayer (mawāqīt al-ṣalāt)	19
The call to prayer (al-adhān); place of the leader, al-imām, with details for movements to be made and words to be repeated	63
The congregational service (al-jum'ah) held on Friday	15
Prayer at time of terror (ṣalāt al-khawf)	3
The feasts (kitāb al-'īdayn), about the two feasts of 'Īd al-Fiṭr at the end of Ramaḍān and 'Īd al-Aḍḥā, when sacrifices are made during the pilgrimage	10
Extra prayer (al-witr)[3]	3
Prayer for rain (al-istisqā')	9
The eclipse (al-kusūf), prayer at the time of eclipses of the sun and moon	8

1. This translation is from the Arabic of *Kitāb al-Jām' al-Ṣaḥīḥ,* the great collection of traditions of al-Bukhārī, *(Le Recueil des Traditions Mahométanes,* Edit. M. L. Krehl, Brill, 1862).

2. A more accurate transliteration is *ṣalāh.*

3. *Enc. of Islam,* Vol. IV, p. 1139.

Qur'ānic worship (sujūd al-Qur'ān), prostration according to the Qur'ān and the sunnah	2
Shortening prayer (taqṣīr al-ṣalāt) for special occasions	6
Prayer at night (al-tahajjud)	15
The excellence of prayer in the shrine of Makkah and al-Madīnah (faḍl al-ṣalāt fī masjid Makkah wa'l-Madīnah)	2
Behavior during prayer (al-'amal fī al-ṣalāt)	7
Negligence (al-sahw)	4
Funerals (al-janā'iz)	39
The poor tax (al-zakāt)	32
The pilgrimage (al-ḥajj), with detailed traditions about its procedure	59
The minor pilgrimage (al-'umrah)	8
Prohibition of and compensation for the hunt (muḥṣar wa-jaza' al-ṣayd), rules for the sacred enclosure at Makkah; two short sections	15
The virtues of al-Madīnah (faḍā'il al-Madīnah)	5
The fast (al-ṣawm)	16
Special Ramaḍān prayer (ṣalāt al-tarāwīḥ)	1
Excellence of the Night of Power (faḍl laylat al-qadr)	2
Ascetic seclusion (al-i'tikāf), religious retreat	6
Tradings (al-buyū'), with traditions about commerce at the time of the Prophet	39
Advance payment (al-salam), with rules for honest dealing in connection with payment and delivery	3
Pre-emption (al-shuf'ah)	1
Hire (al-ijārah)	8
Transfer of debts (al-ḥawālāt)	1
Suretyship (al-kafālah)	4
Agency (al-wakālah)	6
Sharecropping contracts (al-ḥarth wa'l-muzāra'ah)	8
Drinking (al-shurb); rights for use and exploitation of water and milk[4]	8
Borrowing, discharging debts, withholding property and bankruptcy (al-istiqrāḍ wa-adā' al-duyūn wa'l-ḥijr wa'l-taflīs)	6
Litigations (al-khuṣūmāt)	4
Things picked up (al-luqṭah)	4
Injustices and anger (al-maẓālim wa'l-ghaḍab), penalties, forgiveness; examples of unfair treatment	12

4. Wensinck uses the form *al-sharb*.

Partnership (al-shirkah), in agriculture business, etc.	6
Pledges (al-rahn), pawns, mortgages, etc.	2
Manumission (al-'itq); traditions encouraging the freeing of slaves	10
A slave buying his freedom (al-mukātab)	3
The gift (al-hibah), different types for different persons	17
Testimonies (al-shahādāt); witnessings and evidences of misdemeanors	18
Reconciliation (al-ṣulḥ), sometimes with the idea of compromise	6
Conditions (al-shurūṭ) for various contracts	13
Wills (al-waṣāyā); bequests of one third of the estate, gifts to charity, care of legacies for orphans, disposal of debts	13
The holy war (al-jihād); a long passage about all phases of raids in the name of religion	72
Assignment of the fifth part (farḍ al-khums) of the war booty to the Prophet for special purposes	21
The poll tax and truces with the peoples conquered in war (al-jizyah wa'l-muwāda'ah ma' ahl al-dhimmah wa'l-lḥarb)	11
The beginning of creation (bad' al-khalq), traditions about the world, heaven and hell	28
The prophets (al-anbiyā') from Adam to Jesus and Muḥammad	50
The virtues (al-manāqib); traditions about Makkah, Zamzam, the Prophet, etc.	35
Excellent qualities of the Prophet's Companions (faḍā'il aṣḥāb al-Nabī), who accompanied him from Makkah	32
Virtues of the Anṣār (manāqib al-anṣār), or persons of al-Madīnah, who helped the Prophet	48
The raids (al-maghāzī); a long description with traditions about Badr and other battles	136
Exegesis of the Qur'ān (tafsīr al-Qur'ān), with at least one or two traditions forming a commentary about every one of the 114 chapters of the Qur'ān	197
Excellent qualities of the Qur'ān (faḍā'il al-Qur'ān)	19
Marriage (al-nikāḥ); many traditions giving the Prophet's comments about marriage	47
Divorce (al-ṭalāq) with details about rights and procedures	26
Maintenance (al-nafaqāt), or means of support	7
Foods, (al-aṭ'imah); sayings about things to eat, good and bad	20
New birth (al-'aqīqah); traditions about birth and children	1

Sacrifices and hunting (al-dhabā'iḥ wa'l-ṣayd); ordinances for the shrine at Makkah, use of animals slain, methods of hunting, hunting dogs, fishing, victims offered to idols, meats permitted for eating, etc. 56
Victims of sacrifice (al-aḍāḥī); traditions about formalities and occasions for slaughtering animals and use of the meat 7
Drinks (al-ashribah); prohibition of liquor and miscellaneous sayings about drinking 13
The sick (al-marḍā); maladies of different types of persons 9
Medicine (al-ṭibb); use of honey, camel's milk and urine, snuff, cupping, cauterizing, antimony. Leprosy, worms, charms, stomach remedies, pleurisy, fever, plague; incantation, evil eye, auguries, soothsaying, magic; poison, ass' milk, infection from flies, etc. 22
Clothing (al-libās), with traditions about different colors of wearing apparel, what the Prophet approved of, sandals, rings, jewelry, trimming the moustache and beard, perfume, tattoo, harmful designs, etc. 36
Ethical behavior (al-adab); traditions about parents, sympathy for the underprivileged, relationships with neighbors and relatives, helping those in need, conversation, deputations, proper deportment, hospitality, manner of speech, etc. 57
Asking for permission (al-isti'dhān); forms of salutation, giving pardon, salutation in a letter, company manners, keeping a secret and locking up one's house 18
Invocations (al-da'awāt); pious words to be said on all sorts of occasions 25
Slaves (al-riqāq), meaning slaves of Allāh; many sayings about good and bad living, judgment, heaven and hell 40
Divine decree (al-qadr), predestination 7
Oaths and vows (al-aymān wa'l-nudhūr) 20
Expiations for oaths (kaffārāt al-aymān); acts of charity and piety to atone for errors 5
Shares of inheritance (al-farā'iḍ) 10
Restrictive ordinances (al-ḥudūd), with penalties for stealing, adultery and drinking liquor 21
Blood money (al-diyāt); compensation for crimes and injuries, "An eye for an eye," etc. 13
Asking apostates and obstinate people to repent and fighting with them (istitābāt al-murtaddīn wa'l-mu'ānidīn wa-qitāluhum); a few traditions about unbelievers 7

Constraint (al-ikrāh) about agnostics, difficult women, wrong doings, etc. 4

Devices (al-ḥiyal); this might be rendered as legal fiction, but refers more especially to trickery in connection with marriage, trade, labor and other things 7

Interpretation (al-ta'bīr); telling of visions and dreams of the Prophet, Joseph, certain women, etc. Sayings about sleep and interpretation of dreams 18

Tempting away from the truth (al-fitan), with sayings about seduction from right belief, opposition to Islām and destruction of the rebels at the end of the world 17

Precepts (al-aḥkām); many quotations about obedience to the ordinances, the necessity for judgments to be in keeping with Islām, judicial administration, work of the judges and voluntary acceptance of authority 23

Longing (al-tamannī); a few miscellaneous sayings 5

Comments on "singles" (akhbār al-āḥād); traditions quoted only by single persons 6

Avoiding sin with the Book and the sunnah (al-i'tiṣam bi'l-kitāb wa'l-sunnah); sayings to explain how the Qur'ān, together with the words and precedents of the Prophet, can be a means for righteous living. The evil of raising questions about the revelations of Allāh; traditions about Makkah and al-Madīnah; sayings about important persons, etc. 26

Oneness (al-tawḥīd); sayings about Allāh, his uniqueness; his oneness in spite of attributes and hundred names; also sayings about Adam, Noah, Muḥammad's mission and the Qur'ān; long passages important for theologians 56

Appendix III

Summary of the Contents of Kitab al-Umm

Part I

Ritual Purity (al-ṭahārah), 49 pages.[1]

Water which does and does not purify for ablution (al-wuḍū') ; proper vessels for ablution, the prescribed rites; ablution after bowel movements, urine, passing gas, eating and drinking. Washing the hands, face, head and feet; places and numbers of ablutions; when washing is not required; how to make the ablution; ablutions for prayer, times of sickness and journeys; use of sand as a substitute for water; purification after sex intercourse and contact with semen.

Menstruation (al-ḥayḍ), 8 pages.

Abstention from sex intercourse during menstruation; refraining from prayer; technicalities concerning the duration; treatment for blood and other details.

Prayer (al-ṣalāt), 193 pages.

Ordinances for prayer; the five prayers; prayer of drunkards and persons in abnormal mental states; times of prayer, details for regular prayers and prayers during a journey or sickness; detailed instructions for the call to prayer; clothing for prayer; how men and women should pray when robbed of their garments.

The direction (al-qiblah) facing Makkah and conditions for disregarding it; prayer at the Ka'bah.

The intention to pray; the call "Allāh is the greatest" (al-takbīr); reading the Qur'ān at times of prayer. Bodily positions; raising of the hands, kneeling, prostration, etc. Words to be repeated for the ritual of prayer stated in detail.

Prayers for Muḥammad and 'Alī. The hours of prayer; details about the prayer leader (al-imām). Friday prayers; presence of the ruler; prayer in private homes and on journeys; ritual and

1. This summary is based on the great codification of law according to al-Shāfi'ī, known as *Kitāb al-Umm,* edited by al-Rabī' ibn-Sulaymān and printed in Arabic by al-Amīrīyah Press, Cairo, 1903. For a summary in English of al-Ispahānī, see Macdonald *(Dev. Muslim)* pp. 351-357.

rules for the Friday services; the sermon (al-khuṭbah) and readings to accompany it; the night before Friday prayers.

Prayer at times of alarm, danger and war. Prayers for the great feasts; ablutions, food, decorations; the call to prayer, words to be repeated, bodily movements, the sermon, who must attend, etc.

Prayer at times of eclipses and for rain.

Funerals; detailed instructions for washing the corpse; burial during battle; confusion with unbelievers; proper formalities and ceremonial prayers.

Part II

The Alms Tax (al-zakāt), 78 pages.

Rate of the tax for camels, cows, sheep and mixed herds; exemption of horses; where the cattle are to be placed and security for them.

Use of the tax for charity and the orphans, etc.

The tax for palm trees, vineyards, grains, saffron; exemption of honey. The tax for metals, ornaments and treasures. Effect of death in connection with payment; details for taxes on commercial transactions.

Alms and charity gifts at the time of feasts; shares and methods of collection.

The Fast (al-ṣawm), 10 pages.

Instructions for Ramaḍān and other fasts, given in briefer form than the ordinances for prayer and the alms tax. Seclusion (al-i'tikāf), or withdrawal for religious purposes and its connection with fasting.

The Pilgrimage (al-ḥajj), 62 pages.

Persons for whom it is a duty; under what circumstances it is a duty; rules for women and slaves; period of the pilgrimage; the persons exempt.

The lesser pilgrimage (al-'umrah).

Ceremonial ablutions and garments; the interference of enemies; sickness, detailed instructions for rites and prayers at the Ka'bah.

Ordinances about refraining from hunting and what to do with animals, insects and vermin while on the pilgrimage; ostriches and their eggs, wild cows and asses, goats, the hyena, gazelles, the jerboa, fox, giant lizard, cony; birds, locusts, insects and lice.

Instructions for the ceremonies at al-Ṣafā and al-Marwah,

'Arafah and Minā. The animal sacrifice. Menstruation and the pilgrimage.

Further statements about hunting and fishing; Jewish methods of slaughtering the sacrificial victims; forbidden foods; things which Muslims must not eat and drink.

Repetition of rules for the lesser pilgrimage and instructions for the intermediate one. Regulations similar to those of the great pilgrimage; methods of sacrifice and use of votive offerings.

Part III

Commercial Transactions (al-buyū'), 293 pages.

Selections, testimonials; selling of vegetables, fruits, meats, grains, etc. Witnessing a bargain; barter between peasants and nomads; selling of animals, garments, material, wood, leather, etc.

Very detailed instructions for all kinds of loans, guarantees, securities and pledges; loans of persons who die.

Partnership and guardianship.

Deals with persons mentally incapable; decisions concerning ambiguous questions, inheritance, etc. Conditions for slavery and the slave market.

Various agricultural laws; rents, reclamation of land, entailed trusts and limitations.

Varied interpretations of the authorities in different localities about miscellaneous questions. Gifts; small and large things picked up by chance.

Part IV

Shares of Inheritance (al-farā'iḍ), 14 pages.

The heirs determined by the Qur'ān; special cases.

The theory of inheritance; ambiguous cases; many details.

The Will (al-waṣāyā), 65 pages.

Making and cancelling a will or bequest; different kinds of possession and various circumstances affecting a will. Bequests for the indigent, the ascetic, the pilgrim, the freed slave, the sick, etc. Wills refused and changed. Bequest for a wife; bequest of one third of the estate.

Gifts made at sea and during war time.

Question of bequests to heirs and the technicalities involved; bequests to relatives and to babes in the womb; question of a slave set free.

Various modifications of the rules.

Bequest and clientship; the deposit and fulfilment; disposal of women, offspring, horses and booty taken as the spoils of war.

Tribute (al-jizyah), 119 pages.

Taxes to be collected from the People of the Book[2] who refuse to accept Islām.

The holy war (al-jihād) dealt with in detail; treatment of the people of occupied territories; value of the tribute, with methods of collecting and cancelling it. Questions connected with improvement of the land.

Judgments related to the conquered peoples; the killing of aggressors and opponents, idolaters and apostates; remarks about aggression and calamity.

How tribute is affected by war; a child under fifteen exempt from hostile treatment; supplies of the conquered peoples; treatment of conquered women, girls, proselytes and slaves.

Part V

Marriage (al-nikāḥ), 173 pages.

What permits and what prevents intercourse of the sexes.

Marriage with women of the People of the Book; prohibition of marriage with the women of idolaters.

Questions of clientship, guardianship, the insane, childless women, etc.

The marriage contract; women a man may not marry because of close relationship; normal and abnormal cases.

The betrothal; question of marrying slaves; technical problems related to polygamy and proper treatment for a number of wives; treatment of women who are polytheists.

The dowry (al-ṣidāq or al-mahr).

Temporary marriage (al-mut'ah).

Selection of the bride; responsibility for a wife's expenses; varieties and conditions of expenses for journeys, divorce, slaves, etc. Diverse opinions about marriage, divorce, the dowry and betrothal; technicalities connected with menstruation; miscellaneous questions.

Divorce (al-ṭalāq), 126 pages.

Statement of divorce; divorce as connected with the menstrua-

2. Originally Christians, Jews and Ṣābians, but later extended to include Berbers and Zoroastrians.

tion periods; financial aspects of divorce; the wording of a divorce; conditions permitting a wife to withdraw; the period during which a woman cannot remarry (al-'iddah), with questions of pregnancy, menstruation, and the fatherhood of the baby.

Periods of time in connection with death, divorce and remarriage; return of a divorced woman; marriage after a threefold divorce.

Questions of adultery, illness and other causes for separation. The divorce of a client or slave. Certainty and uncertainty in connection with divorce; the period of refraining from sexual intercourse; the declaration of divorce.

Part VI

Injuries with Intention (jirāḥ al-'amd), 89 pages.

Murder and its punishment; types and occasions of murder and the killing of men, women and slaves; details and technicalities. Killing in war time and judgment of the conquered persons.

Lex Talionis for parts of the body, sight, hearing, etc.

Offenses of the sulṭān; indemnities and blood money; offenses against women and slaves.

Indemnities for Unintentional Misdemeanors (dīyāt al-khaṭa'), 23 pages.

The indemnity for an injury to a freeborn Muslim man, for a woman, a hermaphrodite, or for insane persons of different types; release from the blood money.

Rules for injuries to camels, intended and accidental; blood money (al-'aql) for different categories of persons; indemnities for the nose, tongue, eyes, palate, male sex organ of the normal man and of the hermaphrodite, for the head, beard, ears, lips, teeth and breasts.

Punishments (al-ḥudūd), Restrictive Ordinances, 84 pages.

Robbery; punishment of the thief by amputation of the hand or foot. Adultery with its punishment and requirement for witnesses. Alcoholic liquor and penalty for drinking. Beating of a woman; the rod. Highway robbery.

Legal responsibility after puberty when fifteen years old.

Fugitive slaves; cutting off members of their bodies; also the fine for theft; return of an adulterer.

Apostasy, with many details; also the return to faith.

Questions concerning the cupper, circumciser and blacksmith. Beating of an animal to death. Offenses of a Qur'ānic teacher and of a physician.

Drinking at feasts; different points of view regarding clients and slaves; miscellaneous technicalities.

Administration of Justice (al-aqḍīyah), 493 pages.

(This topic continues into Part VII, filling a volume and a half. Only a few general subjects can be mentioned in this summary.) The judge (al-qāḍī), his responsibility and work. Witnesses and details about types of cases. Property divisions; summons and evidence; witnesses for different sorts of personal and commercial cases.

Part VII

Oaths described in detail; the testimonies of persons of different sexes, ages and categories.

Punishments and restrictive ordinances described in great detail; oaths and expiation; perjury; details concerning different types of cases. Making and breaking vows to do various things; vows connected with divorce and orphans.

Testimonies and oaths; circumstantial evidence; details about evidence for sales, farming, charity, security, wills, inheritance, partnership, the freeing of slaves, rents, religious rites, robbery, marriage, divorce, various offenses, etc. Also instructions connected with the manumission of slaves.

A very long passage reviewing the details of subjects already mentioned and the disagreements between the jurists about these matters.

Shares of the estate; the number of slaves to be set free and the number to form part of the estate. Disposal of properties described in detail; written documents and contracts.

Slaves of many types; their sale, manumission and relationship with questions of inheritance and clientship.

Appendix IV

A Summary of the Principal Dogmas of al-Ash'arī as They are Mentioned in Two of his Creeds[1]

The substance of belief is acknowledgment of Allāh, His angels, His books[2] and His apostles, as well as the revelation of Allāh and the truths handed down by trustworthy persons on the authority of Muḥammad.

Allāh is one and Muḥammad is His Apostle. Heaven and hell are both real; the Last Day and the bodily resurrection are coming. Allāh is seated on His throne; He has two hands, two eyes and a face, but we do not ask how.

Allāh has knowledge, hearing, sight and power. His speech is uncreated; there is nothing good or evil except as He wills. No one can do anything before He prescribes it and no one can evade His knowledge, for the acts of creatures are created and determined by Allāh.

Allāh helps believers to obey Him, but leads unbelievers astray, as He has willed that they should not believe and so He abandons them. Men do not possess either good or evil except as Allāh wills.

The Qur'ān is the uncreated speech of Allāh; whoever says that the Qur'ān is created is an unbeliever.

Allāh will be seen by the eyes of the believers in the life to come.

No Muslim is an unbeliever because of a crime which he commits, such as adultery, theft or drinking wine. If, however, he declares that the crime is legal, he is an unbeliever. Allāh will release some people from the fire of hell after they have been burned, because of the intercession of the Apostle Muḥammad.

Men will be punished both in the grave and after their

1. *Maqālāt al-Islāmīyīn* and *Ibānah 'an Uṣūl al-Diyānah*. See Ash'arī *(Theology)* pp. 236-254 and *(Ibānah)* pp. 31-35; 49-55.

2. The Torah, Psalms, Gospels were the most important. Muḥammad was the seal of the prophets, but there were many who preceded him. The "revelation of Allāh" was the Qur'ān.

resurrection. Their records will be weighed on scales and Allāh will settle their accounts, allowing the believers to cross the bridge to heaven.

Faith is speech and work. Disputation and quarrelling about religion is bad; Allāh does not approve of evil or command it, even though He wills it.

The Companions of the Prophet are to be loved and praised. Abū-Bakr was the foremost, then 'Umar, 'Uthmān and 'Alī. These first four caliphs were well directed, rightly guided successors, the best of all men after the Prophet himself. Muslims should pray for their caliphs, abstaining from revolution and civil war.

Allāh descends to the lowest heaven, asking "Is there any one who seeks forgiveness?"

No innovation is to be introduced, as reliance must be placed on the Qur'ān, the sayings and precedents of the Prophet and the consensus of opinion of Muslim scholars.

It is right to pray on Fridays and feast days, following a prayer leader, even if he is not a good man.

It is a duty to fight in the holy war against the polytheists, until the time comes for battle with the Anti-Christ (al-Dajjāl). In the course of time al-Dajjāl will appear and be slain by Jesus, the son of Mary.

The angels, al-Nakīr and al-Munkar, will question persons in their graves.

The story of Muḥammad's ascent to heaven is true. Many visions seen during sleep are true.

Prayer and almsgiving in honor of deceased Muslims bring them benefits from Allāh.

Sorcery truly exists, a sorcerer being an unbeliever. Hell fire and heaven are created.

Death and killing are foreordained. Satan tempts men, placing doubts in their minds. Allāh will send the children of the polytheists to the fire, disposing of other infants as He wills. It is necessary to endure patiently what Allāh ordains, holding fast to what He has commanded and abstaining from what He has forbidden.

Faith involves loyalty to the Muslim community with avoidance of the great sins, as well as of false speaking, sectarianism, boasting, insolence, pride and condemnation of other men. Every summons to innovation must be avoided.

There must be diligence in reciting the Qur'ān, in writing the traditions and in studying the law. There must also be moral and generous well-doing, while refraining from injury, slander and greed for food and drink.

Our help is in Allāh, to Him do we belong and to Him we shall return.

Bibliography

Ahwānī, Aḥmad Fu'ād, *Al-Tarbiyah fī al-Islām* (Dar Iḥyā' al-Kutub al-'Arabīyah, Cairo, 1955).

'Alī, Muḥammad, *A Manual of Hadith* (Maktaba Ahmadiya, Lahore).

Anawātī, (M. M. Qanawātī) and L. Gardet, *Introduction à la Théologie Musulmane* (Librarie Philosophique J. Vrin, 1948).

Arberry, A. J., *Sufism, an Account of the Mystics of Islam* (Allen & Unwin, 1950).

Ash'arī, al-, 'Alī ibn-Ismā'īl, *Al-Ibānah 'an Uṣūl al-Diyānah,* trans., W. C. Klein (Amer. Oriental Soc., 1940).

_____. *The Theology of al-Ash'arī,* edit., R. J. McCarthy (Imprimerie Catholique, Beirut, 1953).

Baghdādī, al-, abū-Manṣūr ibn-Ṭāhir, *Moslem Schisms and Sects,* trans., Kate C. Seelye (Columbia Univ. Press, 1920); Abraham S. Halkin (Tel-Aviv, 1935).

Bahay, Muḥammad, *Al-Ghazzālī fī al-Falsafah al-Akhlāqīyah wa'l-Ṣūfīyah* (Majallat Risālat al-Islām, Vol. VII).

Balādhurī, al-, Aḥmad, *The Origins of the Islamic State,* trans., Philip K. Ḥittī (Columbia Univ. Press, 1916).

Bayḍāwī, al-, 'Abdallāh ibn-'Umar, *Tafsīr al-Qāḍī al-Bayḍāwī* (Dār al-Sa'ādah, 1896).

_____. *Chrestomathia Baidawiana,* trans., D. S. Margoliouth (Luzac, 1894).

Bell, Richard, *Introduction to the Qur'ān* (Edinburgh Univ. Press,, 1953).

Bouman, Johan, *Le Conflit autour du Coran et la Solution d'al-Baqillānī* (Van Campen, Amsterdam, 1959).

Brockelmann, Carl, *History of the Islamic Peoples,* trans., Carmichael and Perlmann (Putnam's, 1947).

_____. *Geschichte der Arabischen Literatur* (Brill, 1943-1949).

Browne, Edward G., *A Literary History of Persia* (Unwin, 1909).

Bukhārī, al-, Muḥammad ibn-Ismā'īl, *El-Bokhārī, Les Traditions Islamiques,* trans., O. Houdas and W. Marçais (Imprimerie Nationale, 1906).

_____. *Kitāb al-Jāmi' al-Ṣaḥīḥ,* edit., M. L. Krehl (Brill, 1862).

———. *Ṣaḥīḥ al-Bukhārī,* edit., al-Kirmānī (al-Miṣrīyah Press, 1934).

Burckhardt, Titus, *Vom Sufitum* (Barth-Verlag, Munich, 1952).

Calverley, Edwin E., *Islam, an Introduction* (American Univ. at Cairo, 1958). *See also* Ghazzālī, al-,

Carra, *see* Vaux, de.

Coon, Carleton, *Caravan* (Henry Holt, 1951).

Cragg, Kenneth, *The Call of the Minaret* (Oxford Univ. Press, 1956).

Creswell, K. A. C., *The Muslim Architecture of Egypt* (Clarendon Press, 1952-1959).

Dā'irat al-Ma'ārif al-Islāmīyah (Cairo, 1932-1952).

Dāwūd, abū-, al-Sijistānī, *Sunun abī-Dāwūd* (al-Kastānīyah Press, Cairo, 1863).

Dodge, Bayard, *Al-Azhar: a Millennium of Muslim Learning* (The Middle East Institute, 1961).

Donaldson, Dwight M., *Studies in Muslim Ethics* (SPCK, London, 1953).

Dozy, R., *Dictionnaire Détaillé des Noms des Vêtements chez les Arabes* (Amsterdam, 1845).

Encyclopaedia of Islam (Brill and Luzac, 1913 ff.)

Faḍl (Mirza abu'l-Fazl) *Sayings of the Prophet Muhammad* (Reform Society, Allahabad, 1924).

Field, Claud, *Mystics and Saints of Islam* (Griffiths, 1910).

Fyzee, Asaf A. A., *Outlines of Muhammadan Law* (Oxford Univ. Press, 1955).

Gaudefroy-Demombynes, Maurice, *Muslim Institutions,* trans., J. P. Macgregor (Allen and Unwin, 1950).

Ghazzālī, al-, abū-Ḥāmid Muḥammad, *The Confessions of al-Ghazzālī,* trans., Claud Field (John Murray, 1909).

———. *Iḥyā' al-'Ulūm* (al-Maymūnīyah Press, Cairo, 1916).

———. *Ih'ya Ouloūm ed-Dīn,* edit., G. H. Bousquet (Max Besson, 1955).

———. *The Faith and Practice of al-Ghazālī,* edit., W. M. Watt (Allen and Unwin, 1953), with translations of *Al-Munqidh min al-Ḍalāl* and *Bidāyat al-Hidāyah.*

———. *O Youth* or *Ayyuha'l-Walad,* edit., George H. Scherer (Amer. Press, Beirut, 1933).

———. *Tahāfut al-Falāsifah,* trans., Ṣabīḥ Ahmad Kamālī (McGill Univ., 1955).

———. *Worship in Islām,* trans., Edwin E. Calverley (Christian Literary Soc., Madras, 1925; Luzac & Co., London, 1957).

Gibb, H. A. R., *Arabic Literature* (Oxford Univ. Press, 1926).

———. *Mohammedanism* (Oxford Univ. Press, 1949).

Goldziher, Ignaz, *Madhāhib al-Tafsīr al-Islāmī,* trans., 'Abd-al-Ḥalīm al-Najjār (al-Khanjī Press, Cairo, 1955).

———. *Muhammedanische Studien* (Max Niemeyer, Halle, 1890).

Guillaume, Alfred, *Islam* (Penguin Books, 1954).

———. *Life of Muhammad* (Oxford Univ. Press, 1955).

———. *The Traditions of Islam* (Clarendon Press, 1924).

Ḥayyān, abū-, *Tafsīr al-Baḥr al-Muḥīṭ* (al-Sa'ādah Press, Cairo, 1910).

Hazard, Harry W., *Atlas of Islamic History* (Princeton Univ. Press, 1954) with aid of H. L. Cooke, Jr.

Heyworth-Dunne, J., *An Introduction to the History of Education in Modern Egypt* (Luzac & Co., London, 1938).

Ḥittī, Philip K., *History of the Arabs* (Macmillan, 1949).

———. *The Arabs; A Short History* (Princeton Univ. Press, 1943).

———. *The Near East in History* (Van Nostrand, 1961).

Ḥusayn, Muḥammad Kāmil, *Dīwān al-Mu'ayyad fī al-Dīn Dā'i al-Du'āh* (Dār al-Kātib al-Miṣrī, 1949).

Iṣbahānī, al-, abū-al-Faraj, *Kītāb al-Aghānī* (Dār al-Ṭibā'ah, Cairo, 1868).

Islām (al-) al-Yawm wa Ghadan (Dār Iḥyā' al-Kutub al-'Arabīyah, Cairo, 1957).

Islamic Culture (Islamic Culture Board, Hyderabad-Deccan, India).

Jalālayn, al-, (Jalāl-al-Dīn al-Maḥallī wa-Jalāl-al-Dīn al-Suyūṭī) *Tafsīr al-Qur'ān al-'Aẓīm* (Dār Iḥyā' al-Kutub al-'Arabīyah, Cairo, 1920).

Jeffery, Arthur, *Materials for the History of the Text of the Qur'ān* (Brill, 1937).

Jubayr, ibn-, abū-al-Ḥusayn Muḥammad, *The Travels of ibn-Jubayr,* edit., M. J. de Goeje (Librarie Orientale et Américaine, 1907).

———. *The Travels of ibn-Jubayr,* trans., R. J. C. Broadhurst (Jonathan Cape, 1952).

Jurjī, Edward J., *Illumination in Islamic Mysticism* (Princeton Univ. Press, 1938).

Khaddūrī, Majīd and H. L. Liebesny, *Law in the Middle East* (Middle East Institute, 1955). *See also* Shāfi'ī, al-.

Khaldūn, ibn-, 'Abd-al-Raḥmān, *Muqaddimat ibn-Khaldūn,* edit., M. Quatremère (Benjamin Duprat, Paris, 1858).

———. *The Muqaddimah,* trans., Franz Rosenthal (Bollingen Series, xliii, Pantheon Books, 1958).

———. *Les Prolégomènes d'Ibn Khaldoun,* trans., M. de Slane, (Imprimerie Impériale, 1863).

Khallikān, ibn-, Aḥmad, *Wafayāt al-A'yān wa-Anbā' Abnā' al-Zamān* (Maymūnīyah Press, Cairo, 1888).

———. *Ibn-Khallikan's Biographical Dictionary,* trans., M. de Slane (Duprat, Paris and Allen & Co., London, 1843).

Lammens, Henri, *Calife Omaiyade Mo'āwia Ier* (Harrassowitz, Leipzig, 1908).

Le Tourneau, Roger, *Fès Avant le Protectorat* (Société Marocaine de Librairie et d'Edition, Casablanca, 1949).

Lyall, Charles J., *Translations of Ancient Arabic Poetry, Chiefly Pre-Islamic* (Columbia Univ. Press, 1930).

Ma'arrī, Abū-al-'Alā', *Luzūmīyāt,* trans., Amīn al-Riḥānī (Ṣādir Riḥānī, Beirut, 1944).

Macdonald, Duncan B., *Development of Muslim Theology, Jurisprudence and Constitutional Theory* (Routledge, 1903) .

———. *The Religious Attitude and Life in Islam* (Univ. of Chicago Press, 1935; reprint Lahore, Pakistan, 1960).

Maḥmaṣānī, Ṣubḥī (S. Mahmassani), *Falsafat al-Tashrī' fī al-Islām,* trans., Farḥāt Ziyādah (Ziadeh), (Brill, 1961).

Maqrīzī, al-, Taqī-al-Dīn Aḥmad, *Kitāb al-Khiṭaṭ al-Maqrīzīyah* (al-Nīl Press, 1906).

———. *Kitāb al-Sulūk li-Ma'rifat Duwal al-Mulūk,* edit., M. Muṣṭafā Ziyādah (Lajnat al-Ta'līf wa'l-Tarjamah wa'l- Nashr, Cairo, 1956-1958) .

Ma'rūf, Nājī, *Al-Madrasah al-Mustanṣirīyah* (Nādī al-Muthannā, Baghdād, 1935).

Massignon, Louis, *Al-Hallaj, Martyr Mystique de l'Islam* (Geuthner, 1922).

Merchant, Muḥammad Valibhai, *A Book of Quranic Laws* (Ashraf, Lahore, 1947).

Mez, Adam, *The Renaissance of Islam,* trans., S. A. Bukhsh and D. S. Margoliouth, (Luzac, 1937).

Muslim ibn al-Ḥajjāj, *Al-Saḥīḥ,* (al-Miṣrīyah Press, 1873).

Muslim World, The, (Hartford Seminary Foundation).

Nadīm, abū-al-Faraj Muḥammad ibn-Isḥāq, known as ibn-abī-Ya'qūb al-Nadīm, *Kitāb al-Fihrist,* edit., Gustav Flügel (Vogel, Leipzig, 1871).

———. *Beatty Manuscript* (Chester Beatty Museum, Dublin).

Nādir, Albert Naṣrī, *Le system Philosophique des Mu'tazila* (Les Lettres Orientales, Beirut, 1956).

Nasafī, al-, 'Abdallāh ibn-Aḥmad, *Tafsīr al-Nasafī* (al-Ḥusaynīyah Press, Cairo, 1925).

Naysabūrī, al-, Muḥammad ibn-'Abdallāh, *Al-Madkhal ilā Ma'rifat al-Iklīl,* edit., James Robson (Royal Asiatic Society, Luzac, 1953).

Nicholson, R. A. *A Literary History of the Arabs* (T. Fisher Unwin. 1923, 1930).

———. *The Mystics of Islam* (Brill, 1914).

———. *Studies in Islamic Mysticism* (Cambridge Univ. Press, 1921).

O'Leary, de Lacy, *Arabic Thought and its Place in History* (Routledge & Kegan Paul, 1954).

———. *How Greek Science Passed to the Arabs* (Routledge & Kegan Paul, 1949).

Patton, Walter M., *Aḥmad ibn Ḥanbal and the Miḥna* (Brill, 1879).

Pellat, Charles, *Le Milieu Baṣrien et la Formation de Ǧāḥiẓ* (Adrien-Maisonneuve, 1953).

Qalqashandī, al-, Aḥmad ibn-al-'Abbās, *Ṣubḥ al-A'shā* (Dār al-Kutub al-Miṣrīyah, 1922).

Qanawātī, *see* Anawātī.

Raḍwān, abū-al-Futūḥ Aḥmad, *Old and New Forces in Egyptian Education* (Columbia Univ. 1951).

Robson, James, *An Introduction to the Science of Tradition* (Luzac, 1953).

Roolvink, E. R., *Historical Atlas of the Muslim Peoples* (Djambatan, Amsterdam, 1957).

Sarton, George, *Introduction to the History of Science* (Carnegie Inst. of Washington, 1927).

Schacht, Joseph. *The Origins of Muhammadan Jurisprudence* (Clarendon Press, 1950).

Shāfi'ī, al-, Muḥammad ibn-Idrīs, *Kitāb al-Umm,* edit., al-Rabī' ibn-Sulaymān (al-Amīrīyah Press, Cairo, 1903).

———. *al-Risālah,* trans., Majīd Khaddūrī, with title *Islamic Jurisprudence* (Johns Hopkins Press, 1961).

Shahrastānī, al-, Muḥammad ibn-'Abd-al-Karīm, *Kitāb al-Milal wa'l-Niḥal,* Part II, edit., W. Cureton (Harrassowitz, Leipzig, 1923).

Shalabī (Ahmad Shallaby), *History of Muslim Education* (Dār al-Kashshāf, Beirut, 1954).

Sha'rānī, al- (Cheikh El-Cha'rānī), *Balance de la Loi Musulmane*, trans., Perron (Imprimerie Orientale, Alger, 1898).

Suyūṭī, al-, Jalāl-al-Dīn, *Ḥusn al-Muḥāḍarah fī Akhbār Miṣr wa'l-Qāhirah* (al-Mawsu'āt Press, Cairo) . *See also Jalālayn.*

Ṭabarī, al-, Muḥammad ibn-Jarīr, *Annales,* edit., M. J. de Goeje Brill, 1883-1884).

——. *Tafsīr al-Qur'ān* (Dār al-Ma'ārif, Cairo, 1958).

——. *Tarjamat al-Imām Muḥammad ibn-Jarīr al-Ṭabarī* (al-Maynanīyah Press, Cairo).

Taftāzānī, al-, Sa'd-al-Dīn, *A Commentary on the Creed of Islam,* trans., E. E. Elder (Columbia Univ. Press, 1950).

Ṭahanāwī, al-, Muḥammad, *The Logic of the Arabians,* trans., A. Sprenger (Bengal Military Orphan Press, 1854).

Ṭalas, Asad, *La Madrasa Nizamiyya et son Histoire* (Geuthner, 1939).

Ṭawīl, al-, Tawfīq, *Al-Taṣawwuf fī Miṣr ibbān al-'Āṣr al-'Uthmānī* (al-I'timād Press, Cairo, 1946).

Ṭawṭaḥ (Khalil A. Totah), *The Contribution of the Arabs to Education* (Columbia Univ., 1926).

Tritton, A. S., *Islam: Belief and Practices* (Hutchinson's Univ. Library, 1951).

——. *Materials on Muslim Education in the Middle Ages* (Luzac, 1957).

——. *Muslim Theology* (Luzac, 1947).

Vaux, de-, Carra, *Les Penseurs de l'Islam* (Geuthner, 1921).

von Grunebaum, G. E., *Islam, Essays in the Nature and Growth of a Cultural Tradition* (Amer. Anthropological Assn., 1955).

——. *Medieval Islam* (Univ. of Chicago Press, 1953). *See* Zarnūjī, al-.

Watt, W. Montgomery, *Free Will and Predestination in Early Islam* (Luzac, 1948) . *See also* Ghazzālī, al-.

Wehr, Hans, *Al-Ġazzālī's Buch vom Gottvertrauen* (Max Niemeyer, Halle, 1940).

Wensinck, A. J., *A Handbook of Early Muhammadan Tradition* (E. J. Brill, 1927).

——. *The Muslim Creed* (Cambridge Univ. Press, 1932).

Yāqūt, ibn-'Abdallāh, *Irshād al-Arīb ilā Ma'rifat al-Adīb,* edit., D. S. Margoliouth (Luzac, 1907 ff.), also referred to as *Mu'jam al-Udabā'.*

Zahrah, abū-, Muḥammad, *Al-Shāfi'ī* (Dār al-Fikr al-'Arabī, Cairo, 1948).

Zarnūjī, al-, Burhān-al-Dīn, *Ta'līm al-Muta'allim—Ṭarīq at-Ta'allum,* trans., G. E. von Grunebaum and T. M. Abel (King's Crown Press, New York, 1947).

Zarqā, al, Muṣṭafā, paper issued at the International Islamic Colloquium, Lahore, 1958.

Ziyādah (Farhat J. Ziadeh), *see* Mahmasānī.

Ziyādah (Nicola A. Ziadeh), *Sanūsīyah* (Brill, 1958).

Index

www.ingramcontent.com/pod-product-compliance
Ingram Content Group UK Ltd.
Pitfield, Milton Keynes, MK11 3LW, UK
UKHW021408190726
13845UKWH00028B/957

9 789366 081021